THE COMPETITIVE ADVANTAGE OF COMMON SENSE

Using the
Power You
Already Have

ISBN 0-13-141143-8

In an increasingly competitive world, it is quality
of thinking that gives an edge—an idea that opens new
doors, a technique that solves a problem, or an insight
that simply helps make sense of it all.

We work with leading authors in the various arenas
of business and finance to bring cutting-edge thinking
and best learning practice to a global market.

It is our goal to create world-class print publications
and electronic products that give readers
knowledge and understanding which can then be
applied, whether studying or at work.

To find out more about our business
products, you can visit us at www.ft-ph.com

THE COMPETITIVE
ADVANTAGE OF
COMMON
SENSE

Using the
Power You
Already Have

FERGUS O'CONNELL

FT Prentice Hall

FINANCIAL TIMES

An Imprint of PEARSON EDUCATION

Upper Saddle River, NJ • New York • London • San Francisco • Toronto • Sydney
Tokyo • Singapore • Hong Kong • Cape Town • Madrid
Paris • Milan • Munich • Amsterdam

www.ft-ph.com

Library of Congress Cataloging-in-Publication Data

O'Connell, Fergus.
   The competitive advantage of common sense:using the power you already have/Fergus O'Connell.
      p. cm. -- (Financial Times Prentice Hall books)
   Includes bibliographical references and index.
   ISBN 0-13-141143-8
    1. Executive ability--Problems, exercises, etc. 2. Common sense--Problems, exercises,
   etc. 3. Simplicity--Problems, exercises, etc. 4. Management--Problems, exercises, etc. I.
   Title. II. Series.

HD38.2.O29 2003
658.4'09--dc21

                       2003040592

Editorial/Production Supervisor: *Vanessa Moore*
Full-Service Production Manager: *Anne R. Garcia*
Manufacturing Manager: *Alexis Heydt-Long*
Executive Editor: *Jim Boyd*
Editorial Assistant: *Linda Ramagnano*
Marketing Manager: *John Pierce*
Interior Designer: *Gail Cocker-Bogusz*
Cover Designer Director: *Jerry Votta*
Cover Designer: *Talar Boorujy*

 © 2003 Pearson Education, Inc.
Publishing as Financial Times Prentice Hall
Upper Saddle River, NJ 07458

Authorized adaptation from the original UK edition, entitled
SIMPLY BRILLIANT, First Edition by Fergus O'Connell,
published by Pearson Education Limited, © Pearson Education Limited 2001.

Prentice Hall books are widely used by corporations and government agencies for
training, marketing, and resale.

For information regarding corporate and government bulk discounts please contact:
Corporate and Government Sales (800) 382-3419 or
corpsales@pearsontechgroup.com

Printed in the United States of America

10 9 8 7 6 5 4 3 2 1

ISBN 0-13-141143-8

Pearson Education LTD.
Pearson Education Australia PTY, Limited
Pearson Education Singapore, Pte. Ltd.
Pearson Education North Asia Ltd.
Pearson Education Canada, Ltd.
Pearson Educación de Mexico, S.A. de C.V.
Pearson Education—Japan
Pearson Education Malaysia, Pte. Ltd.

Financial Times Prentice Hall Books

For more information, please go to www.ft-ph.com

Investments

Harry Domash
Fire Your Stock Analyst! Analyzing Stocks on Your Own

Philip Jenks and Stephen Eckett, Editors
The Global-Investor Book of Investing Rules: Invaluable Advice from 150 Master Investors

Charles P. Jones
Mutual Funds: Your Money, Your Choice. Take Control Now and Build Wealth Wisely

D. Quinn Mills
Buy, Lie, and Sell High: How Investors Lost Out on Enron and the Internet Bubble

John Nofsinger and Kenneth Kim
Infectious Greed: Restoring Confidence in America's Companies

John R. Nofsinger
Investment Blunders (of the Rich and Famous)…And What You Can Learn from Them

John R. Nofsinger
Investment Madness: How Psychology Affects Your Investing…And What to Do About It

Leadership

Jim Despain and Jane Bodman Converse
And Dignity for All: Unlocking Greatness through Values-Based Leadership

Marshall Goldsmith, Vijay Govindarajan, Beverly Kaye, and Albert A. Vicere
The Many Facets of Leadership

Frederick C. Militello, Jr., and Michael D. Schwalberg
Leverage Competencies: What Financial Executives Need to Lead

Eric G. Stephan and Wayne R. Pace
Powerful Leadership: How to Unleash the Potential in Others and Simplify Your Own Life

Management

Dr. Judith M. Bardwick
Seeking the Calm in the Storm: Managing Chaos in Your Business Life

J. Stewart Black and Hal B. Gregersen
Leading Strategic Change: Breaking Through the Brain Barrier

William C. Byham, Audrey B. Smith, and Matthew J. Paese
Grow Your Own Leaders: How to Identify, Develop, and Retain Leadership Talent

David M. Carter and Darren Rovell
On the Ball: What You Can Learn About Business from Sports Leaders

Subir Chowdhury
Organization 21C: Someday All Organizations Will Lead this Way

Subir Chowdhury
The Talent Era: Achieving a High Return on Talent

James W. Cortada
Making the Information Society: Experience, Consequences, and Possibilities

Ross Dawson
Living Networks: Leading Your Company, Customers, and Partners in the Hyper-connected Economy

Robert B. Handfield, Ph.d, and Ernest L. Nichols
Supply Chain Redesign: Transforming Supply Chains into Integrated Value Systems

*This book is dedicated
to the memory of Donal McHugh.*

CONTENTS

3

THERE IS ALWAYS A SEQUENCE OF EVENTS   29

4

Things Don't Get Done If People Don't Do Them   55

5
THINGS RARELY TURN OUT AS EXPECTED   95

6
THINGS EITHER ARE OR THEY AREN'T   109

7
LOOK AT THINGS FROM OTHERS' POINTS OF VIEW 119

PREFACE

Much of my adult life has been spent rubbing shoulders with smart people. In college, in every job I've ever had, and in starting my own company, these smart people have been colleagues, bosses, and peers. Because my own background is in software development, many of these smart people have been at home in that discipline—a science that is immensely sophisticated, meticulous, and complicated. I am not alone in this regard, as more and more of us are finding our lives affected by these same smart people and the things they make and do.

Over the years, a suspicion has gradually been growing within me. It is a suspicion that I have been slow to voice. However, as the years have gone by, and as the evidence has accumulated, I have finally come to the conclusion that despite smartness, expertise, skill, experience, and genius, some people are lacking an essential skill: common sense.

"The trouble with common sense," the old saying goes, "is that it's not all that common." That has very much been my experience. Despite all the smarts that are floating around, many dumb things get done. These are things that, if we only applied some of this pixie dust we call common sense, would never have been allowed to happen.

It is against this background that I have written this little book. It tries to set down a number of what one might grandly call "principles" of common sense. Rather than trying to define common sense, it tries to identify practices and principles that, if followed, lead us toward using common sense.

I don't see these principles as being in any way absolute. Another writer might have put forward a different set. However, I believe the principles given here can serve as a useful toolbox for attacking many of the problems that one encounters every day, be it at work or outside of it. Within work, I believe the application of these ideas will yield real benefits—hence, the book's title.

To put things another way, this book might not be the only game in town, but it is a *possible* bag of pixie dust.

ACKNOWLEDGMENTS

This book is a project that I have been nursing for a number of years. I think there was a part of me that always thought it was too wacky for any publisher to be interested in. I would talk to people about it and—it might have been my imagination—they would smile uncomfortably and begin to move warily away. That it has finally seen the light of day is the result of one woman's belief in and passion for the project. That woman is my editor at Pearson Education, Rachael Stock. When Rachael called me to say everyone loved the book proposal, I think what she was really saying was that everyone had been infected by her enthusiasm for it. Rachael has been the perfect editor and I thank her for giving me the chance to write the book.

I would never have gotten to be a writer at all if it hadn't been for Viki Williams, now also at Pearson Education. Viki played an unsung part in this book.

I learned a great lesson in common sense from Paula McHugh. John Brackett of Boston University taught me that things either are or they aren't. Dee Carri and Kevin Barrett at Elan Corporation are both major exponents of the art of common sense. (People whom I call "magicians," Kevin calls "gladiators" and I have used his terminology in Chapter 4.) My colleague, longtime friend, and serious common-sense practitioner Petra Costigan-Oorthuijs created the strip board example in Figure 4.7. My partner Clare Forbes offered advice that was both wise and practical about the structure of the book and its chapters. If the book turns out to be usable, rather than ending up as shelfware, it will be in no small measure due to her suggestions. My colleagues at ETP—Mary Barry, Noel Kelly, Elaine Moore, Conor McCabe,

Bernadette Coleman, Sean McEvoy and Harriet Cotter—all gave valuable input as to what should go into the book.

Three people who taught me much of what I know about common sense are Bernadette, Hugh, and Ferga. Thanks (again), guys.

Jim Boyd, Gail Cocker-Bogusz, Anne Garcia, Vanessa Moore, and Jerry Votta did an outstanding job of preparing this edition for publication. They were creative, meticulous, and a pleasure to work with.

INTRODUCTION

This book identifies what might grandly be called "principles" of common sense. I'd rather think of it as giving a set of ideas—seven of them—that, if you apply, indicate that you are using common sense.

In keeping with the first of the seven ideas—that many things are simple—the book itself is simple. There are seven chapters, one for each of the ideas. Each chapter follows the same organization:

- There are some multiple-choice questions to get you thinking. In a sense, these questions test whether and how much you think in a commonsense manner.

- There is a spiel describing the particular idea.

- Next come some tools to help you apply the idea.

- There are then examples of applying the particular idea. Sometimes the examples are simple applications of the particular idea. Other examples take several of the ideas and combine them.

- Finally, there are some action points or things you could do to begin applying a particular idea in your daily life.

I'd like to know if you find this book useful or if it made any kind of difference—or not! With that in mind, you can e-mail me at *fergus.oconnell@etpint.com* with praise, criticism, or anything in between.

Finally, a note on terminology: I use the words *project*, *venture*, and *undertaking* interchangeably in this book. They all are taken to mean something that you're trying to accomplish.

1

MANY THINGS
ARE SIMPLE

This chapter, together with Chapter 7, acts as bookends to the other chapters. This one extols the virtues of simplicity in our thinking and encourages us to seek out simple solutions.

Questions

1. Somebody who works for you has a major body odor problem. Several of your other people have complained about it. What do you do?

   (a) Send out some vaguely phrased memos about things like "dress code," "grooming," and so on, and see if they take the hint.

   (b) Take them aside, tell them what the problem is, and ask them to do something about it.

   (c) Hand the issue over to human resources.

   (d) Do (a) and if that doesn't work, launch—in conjunction with human resources—a major dress code and grooming initiative that you hope will end up solving both this and any similar or related problems.

2. You have the feeling that your customer service (or customer relationship management [CRM]) is not what it was, or not as good as that of your competitors. What do you do?

   (a) Send people to CRM training courses.

   (b) Begin a major CRM initiative within your company.

   (c) Bring in consultants.

   (d) Ask your people to treat each customer as though they were a friend; that is, somebody who is proud of you and somebody you would not want to let down.

3. It has become trendy and so your people have received some project management training. As part of the package, the project management training company has provided a follow-up mentoring service that works like this: Each course attendee is assigned a mentor at the project management training company. When your people have a project management problem, they simply e-mail their mentor with the problem and a response comes back within

a set time. The training company also provides a summary of the mentoring activity to you to show the value this service is adding. Which of the following is likely to happen?

(a) The mentoring service is overwhelmed with e-mail.

(b) The mentoring service gets a few e-mails at the beginning and then these tail off.

(c) The mentoring service gets no e-mail.

(d) The mentoring service turns out to be useless because the advice is academic rather than practical and real world.

Answers

1. (a) 2 points

Might solve the problem. It'll probably take at least an hour of your time, because the delicate phrasing required will take a good bit of writing and rewriting.

(b) 5 points

Only five minutes and the problem is almost certainly solved. Works for me.

(c) 1 point

Might solve the problem, but now you've got at least two people involved. How much time is going to get consumed putting all of this together?

(d) 0 points

No. Come on, now. You can't be serious.

2. (a) 1 point

Can't hurt. Unless the training is truly execrable, some of it is bound to rub off.

(b) 3 points

Can't hurt either.

(c) 3 points

(Maybe) can't hurt either. It'll hurt your pocketbook, though.

(d) 5 points

If you could *really* get them to do this, in my view, you would have solved all of your CRM problems in a single stroke.

3. (a) 0 points

 I don't think so.

(b) 1 point

Perhaps more likely.

(c) 5 points

This gets my vote. People respond to what gets measured. If they know that you know what level of mentoring they're getting, then you know what level of mentoring they need, and therefore—as they see it—you know how inadequate they are. They won't contact the mentor at all, thereby proving what great project managers they are! Now, you might argue that I am breaching my own idea here, that many things are simple. You might argue that I am being positively Machiavellian. I would not say so. The notion that people respond to what gets measured is a simple concept, readily observable in the real world. Witness the number of people who work late so that they won't go home before the boss.

(d) 4 points

Very likely.

Scores

12–15 points   You have a nice, simple way of looking at the world. (I mean this as a compliment.)

5–11 points   Don't make things more complicated than they are.

Less than 4 points   Read the rest of this chapter.

The Idea

I'll freely accept that some things in life are not simple. Putting a man on the moon, for example, or the *Apollo 13* rescue, were—I'm sure—immensely complex feats of engineering, mathematics, computing, rocketry, and many other disciplines.

However, something you might have come across is the expression "It's not rocket science." Launching, flying, and returning the space shuttle *is* rocket science and requires the application of much complex scientific and technological thought. However, most of us aren't NASA flight directors, and the things we do are definitely not rocket science. Too often, I believe we look for complex solutions when simple ones would be (a) much more appropriate, (b) much easier to find, and (c) much simpler to implement.

Let's look at a few examples of complex solutions.

The Problem of Overly Complex

Here's a little test you could try. In an Internet search engine, type in the phrase *overly complex*. When I did this in Google, I was astonished to get 257,000 results returned. Here are just a few of them:

> "SIU Prof Thinks Overly Complex Legal System Could Collapse." The article goes on to say that "America's legal system could well collapse under its own weight . . . The pace of growth in law is going through the roof . . . It's getting more complicated and top-heavy, you can't do good for any part of society without causing bad for others, and no one knows what's

going on. When we get to the point where people can't understand the law and can't afford help to understand the law, good people will just give up and stop obeying it. When laws don't work, the reverberations are severe."

"Better Institutions Key to Poverty Reduction in Africa and Around the Globe." "Overly complex regulations are especially problematic in poor countries," says Roumeen Islam, director of the World Development Report 2002. "Despite some successful reforms in the Africa region, many countries are left out of market opportunities because of overly complex rules and regulations. For markets to work for everyone, further simplification of institutions and more emphasis on innovative programs that complement existing informal systems are needed."

"Lawmaker Blasts Privacy Notices as Overly Complex." "A high-ranking member of the House Banking Committee recently flogged many of the federally mandated privacy notices crafted by financial service enterprises for being too complex and burdensome for the average citizen."

Is overcomplexity a widespread problem? It looks like it could be!

The Design of Computer Systems

I think you'll agree that the design of most of the computer systems you come across is pretty lousy. (In fact, you could extend this discussion to a whole host of other modern technological wonders—TV remote controls spring to mind—but let's stay focused.) In his wonderful book, *The Inmates Are Running The Asylum* [1], Alan Cooper says that software vendors don't know how to make their programs simple to use, but they sure know how to add features, so that is what they do.

My own business is project management, and the availability of software products such as Microsoft Project, which don't require a

Cray 2 to run on, should have made my life easier. Have they? Anything but. That particular product is difficult and nonintuitive to use, so I still end up relying on bits of paper. Microsoft could do the world a great favor by providing a slimmed-down, elementary, simple set of features that just do the bare essentials. Instead, as each new release comes from the Microsoft factory, we see more and more complex features added.

Tools

If you are ever lucky enough to hear Eli Goldratt speak, he will almost certainly tell you what he calls "one of the fundamental beliefs of science." As he puts it, "In reality there are no complex systems" or "reality cannot be complex." Therefore, our first principle of common sense says that you need to shun complexity and seek simplicity. The following can all help you to do this:

- Look for simple solutions by asking what the simplest thing to do would be in a given situation.

- Ask simple questions: Who? What? Why? Where? When? How?

- Ask for simple answers. This is particularly important when you are dealing with highly technical people.

- Try to describe something—an issue, a problem, a solution, a proposal—coherently in 25 words or less.

- Can you describe that same thing in just 30 seconds? This is sometimes called the "elevator story" or "elevator pitch," the idea being that you meet some important person in an elevator and you've got the travel time of the elevator to convey your message.

- Write down the issue, problem, solution, or proposal. If you find you have ended up with a complex solution or idea, you have probably gone in the wrong direction. Go back and look again, this time in the simple direction.

- When you come up with something, ask if there is a simpler way.

- Get people to tell it to you as if you're a six-year-old.

- Remember the acronym KISS (keep it simple, stupid).

- Learn—and use—lateral thinking. The need for lateral thinking arises out of the way the mind works. The mind acts to create, recognize, and use patterns, but it does not act to *change* patterns. Lateral thinking is all about changing patterns. It is about escaping from old ideas and generating new ones. Lateral thinking involves two basic processes:

  - Escape: recognizing the current received wisdom with regard to something and then searching for alternative ways to look at or do that thing.

  - Provocation: finding those alternative ways.

- Learn to think like Leonardo da Vinci. In a book titled *How to Think Like Leonardo Da Vinci* [2], Michael Gelb identifies what he calls "the fundamentals of Leonardo's approach to learning and the cultivation of intelligence." He crystallizes these in seven principles:

  - Curiosità: Being constantly curious about life and open to new learning.

  - Dimostrazione: Testing knowledge through experience, persistence, and learning from mistakes.

  - Sensazione: Continually refining the senses (sight, hearing, smell, taste, and touch) as a means of enhancing the experience of life.

- Sfumato: In Italian it means "going up in smoke." It refers to being able to be comfortable with paradox, uncertainty, and ambiguity.

- Arte/Scienze: Developing whole-brain thinking (i.e., the balance between art and science, logic and the imagination).

- Corporalita: It's the healthy body part of "a healthy mind in a healthy body" (sana in corpore sano). It's about cultivating grace, fitness, poise, and ambidexterity.

- Connessione: Recognizing that everything is connected to everything else. (As da Vinci put it, "The earth is moved from its position by the weight of a tiny bird resting upon it.")

Examples

Example 1: Running a Successful Business

How do you run a successful business? They say it's complicated. There are business schools out there to enable you do it properly. All manner of complex research has been done in the area. Could you describe it in five minutes, in a page, or in a sentence?

You actually could, and Eileen Shapiro does precisely that in her book, *The Seven Deadly Sins of Business* [3]. She describes the professor entering her first finance class in business school and saying to the wanna-be investment bankers and corporate executives, "Don't run out of cash." The recipe for a successful business? You bet it is.

Example 2: Marketing

Before I started my own company, I used to think that marketing was about sharp suits, power lunches, advertising hype, and being nice to potential customers. I now realize it's one of the most complex, precise, and demanding disciplines on earth. The key to being good at marketing is to be able to explain—very simply—why someone should buy what you sell. If you can tell it to me like I'm a six-year-old, then you will be a great marketeer.

Example 3: Lateral Thinking

There's a story I heard—it might be apocryphal, but even if it is, it serves our purposes well at this point. It goes as follows.

A major U.S. corporation built a new, high-rise corporate headquarters. A few weeks after the building was fully occupied, the employees began to complain about the slowness of the elevators. Very quickly, the complaints reached epidemic proportions, so the company spoke to the architects of the building. Could the elevators be sped up or increased in size? Sure, came the reply, but it would involve months of demolition, extension, and reconstruction around the elevator shafts. It would be hugely disruptive to a large part of the workforce.

Supposedly, the story goes, the corporation did nothing to the elevator shafts. Instead, it placed full-length mirrors on every floor beside the elevator doors. The employees spent an extra few moments preening themselves and looking at one another in the mirrors and the complaints faded.

The point of the story? There must be a simple solution.

So What Should You Do?

1. Look for simple solutions by asking, "What would be the simplest thing to do here?"

2. Ask simple questions: Who? What? Why? Where? When? How? Which?

3. Ask for simple answers. This is particularly important when you are dealing with highly technical people.

4. Try to describe something—an issue, a problem, a solution, a proposal—coherently in 25 words or less.

5. Can you describe that same thing in just 30 seconds? This is sometimes called the "elevator story" or "elevator pitch," the idea being that you meet some important person in an elevator and you've got the travel time of the elevator to convey your message.

6. Write down the issue, problem, solution, or proposal. If you find you have ended up with a complex solution or idea, you have probably gone in the wrong direction. Go back and look again, this time in the simple direction.

7. When you come up with something, ask if there a simpler way.

8. Get people to tell it to you as if you're a six-year-old.

9. Remember the acronym KISS (keep it simple, stupid).

10. Read Edward De Bono's book, *Simplicity* [4].

11. Read any of Edward De Bono's books on lateral thinking, for example, *Lateral Thinking for Management* [5].

12. Read Gelb's *How to Think Like Leonardo Da Vinci* [2].

PRINCIPLE 1: MANY THINGS ARE SIMPLE

References

1. Cooper, Alan, *The Inmates Are Running the Asylum*, Indianapolis, Indiana: SAMS, 1999, p. 27.

2. Gelb, Michael, *How to Think Like Leonardo Da Vinci*, London: Thorsons, 1998, p. xiii.

3. Shapiro, Eileen, *The Seven Deadly Sins of Business*, Oxford, England: Capstone, 1998.

4. De Bono, Edward, *Simplicity*, London: JMW Group, 1990.

5. De Bono, Edward, *Lateral Thinking for Management*, London: Penguin, 1990.

2

KNOW WHAT YOU'RE TRYING TO DO

This chapter makes the age-old point that if you don't know what port you're sailing to, then any wind is a fair wind.

Questions

1. Somebody asks you to come to a meeting "just in case we need your input." What should you do?

   (a) Refuse, on the basis that if they can't tell you the objective and your part in achieving that objective, it's pointless for you to be there.

   (b) See who is is asking you to come. A request from a senior higher-up is much different from a request from one of your peers. Go, if it's a higher-up; refuse on the same grounds as in (a) if it's a peer.

   (c) Go regardless—it comes with the territory.

   (d) Go regardless, but bring your inbox with you so you can get some useful work done.

2. Your company has landed a big project for a client. There is huge pressure to get the project completed on time. What's your first move?

   (a) Send the troops in and tell them to start work.

   (b) Agree with the client (in writing) on completion criteria for the project; that is, how will we *both* know when this project is over and that we have done a good job.

   (c) Definitely don't do (b) on the basis that it will tie you down too much.

   (d) Definitely don't do (b) on the basis that you don't have the time to waste on something you all know anyway.

3. You've nearly completed an order for a customer when he phones you to ask for one small little extra, but still wants delivery when originally agreed. The one little extra is actually reasonably significant. You are new to the company. The customer tells you that your predecessor always accommodated such requests. What do you do?

(a) Say yes. Satisfying the customer is what it's all about.

(b) Ask the team to work some nights and weekends and gripe with them about the "damn customers."

(c) Try to accommodate his desire for the end date not to change by adding more resources. If this fails, tell him the new end date.

(d) Use some of your contingency—assuming you have some— to satisfy the request.

Answers

1. (a) 5 points

This is my favorite.

(b) 5 points

I fully respect your position if you choose this one.

(c) 0 points

I was going to give you 1 point for this, but in thinking about it, you really don't deserve any points for frittering your time away like this.

(d) 1 point

I'll give you 1 point for this (he said softheartedly).

2. (a) 0 points

Lots of people do it, but it isn't the right answer.

(b) 5 points

Yes.

(c) 0 points

Nope. See also the answer to (a).

(d) 0 points

Nope. See also the answer to (a).

3. (a) 0 points

No. No. No. Of course it's about satisfying the customer, but not at this price.

(b) 0 points

Or this. This is the same as (a).

(c) 5 points

Yes. It's not your job to be a magician.

(d) 5 points

Yes, but make a bit of a deal out of it. You were able to do this for him only because you were smart enough to put in contingency in the first place.

Scores

15 points   It's easy to get top marks here.

10–14 points   If you didn't get this far, I'd be a bit concerned that you sometimes aren't focused clearly on what needs to be done.

Less than 10 points   Maybe you don't even *know* what needs to be done!

The Idea

The sentiment is so well known as to be a cliché. The quote is attributed to many different people. To the best of my knowledge it is not clear to whom attribution should go, other than the fact that it was uttered a long time ago. "If you don't know what port you're sailing to," the quote goes, conjuring up visions of sunny sea journeys in an unpolluted and empty Mediterranean, "then any wind is a fair wind."

Put more mundanely, if you don't know what you're trying to do, it's going to be hard to do it. Or let's have it from Lewis Carroll in *Alice's Adventures in Wonderland* [1]. Alice asks the Cheshire Cat, "Would you tell me, please, which way I ought to go from here?"

"That depends a good deal on where you want to get to," says the Cat.

"I don't much care where," says Alice.

"Then, it doesn't matter which way you go," says the Cat.

Whether it's a meeting, a presentation, a day, a week, a year, a life, a house renovation, an ambition, or anything else, if you don't know what you're trying to achieve with it, it's going to be hard to do it.

If you start a meeting and don't know what you're trying to get out of it, the chances of you actually getting something useful, never mind something you actually wanted, from it are pretty remote. At the other end of the scale, you've got one life. If, toward the end of it, you conclude that it wasn't the life you really wanted, it's too late.

It is before dawn as I write this page. When the sun comes up and the day begins, what am I hoping to achieve? What am I trying to accomplish with this day? If I don't know, the day will be happy enough to just pass me by. There is nothing wrong with that necessarily, except that if enough days simply pass by, that could be an entire lifetime.

Tools

In knowing what you are trying to do there are really three issues you have to concern yourself with:

- Understanding what you're trying to do

- Knowing if what you're trying to do is what everyone wants

- Knowing if what you're trying to do has changed

There is also one other tool I'd like to talk about: the notion of visualization.

Understand What You're Trying to Do

Somebody—your boss, say, or a customer—asks you to do something and you start to do it immediately. Right? Uh uh. Bad move.

What you really want to do, before you do anything else, is to understand *precisely* what they've asked you to do. The way to do this is to ask yourself these seven questions:

- How will we know when we're finished?

- What point in time constitutes its end point?

- What physical things will it produce?

- How will the quality of those things be determined?

- What things are definitely part of this?

- What things are definitely *not* part of this?

- Are there any people issues that we need to be aware of in connection with this issue?

Doing this gives you a much clearer picture of what you've been asked to do. It also often points the way forward in terms of what the next moves are.

Know If What You're Trying to Do Is What Everyone Wants

Once you've figured out what it is you think you're trying to do, a good way to check on it is to do what is known as maximizing the win conditions of the stakeholders [2]. It's a fine phrase, but what does it actually mean? Let's parse it from the end and see if we can find out.

The "stakeholders" are all of those people who are going to be affected by what you're proposing to do. Each of those stakeholders has a set of one or more "win conditions," or results that they would like to see emanate from the venture. Finally, "maximizing the win conditions" means trying to find a result that gets the maximum amount of happiness for all of the stakeholders involved in the venture. You can think of understanding what you're trying to do as finding a *possible* outcome to the undertaking, but this is about trying to find the *best* outcome.

We see this notion again in Chapter 7.

Know If What You're Trying to Do Has Changed

Things change. What was important yesterday might not be important today; or somebody might have changed his or her mind about something; or the industry or the business climate or the world changed; or somebody forget something or didn't quite specify it correctly. You need to be watching for such changes to ensure that what you're doing—no matter how laudable it might have been in the past—hasn't suddenly been affected by one of these changes.

Perhaps the best way to do this is to go through the previous two procedures every day. This way, you increase your chances of catching changes and you have an early warning system with a maximum gap of 24 hours before you spot that something is not quite right.

Visualization

Visualization is all about trying to imagine what things will be like. Maybe, in some ways, daydreaming is a better word. Visualization is a powerful technique because it forces you to see what you're trying to do from many different perspectives. It can have dramatic and wide-ranging effects. In particular, visualizing what you're trying to do can have the following effects:

- It helps you to identify the goal of a project or venture in the first place.

- It tightens definition of that goal, identifying things that lie within the scope of the venture and things that fall outside it.

- As we will see in the next example, it starts the planning process—the transition from the what (we are doing) to the how (we will do it).

- It can be a huge motivator to all of those involved in the project, as we paint the picture of where we are heading, what we will have achieved when we get there, and what the journey there will be like.

Here's a great example of visualization taken from Martin Luther King Jr.'s Washington, DC, speech in 1963:

> I say to you today, my friends, so even though we face the difficulties of today and tomorrow, I still have a dream. It is a dream deeply rooted in the American meaning of its creed, "We hold these truths to be self-evident, that all men are created equal." I have a dream that one day on the red hills of Georgia, sons of former slaves and sons of former slave owners will be able to sit down together at the table of brotherhood. I have a dream that one day even the state of Mississippi, a state sweltering with the heat of injustice, sweltering with the heat of oppression, will be transformed into an oasis of freedom and justice. I have a dream that my four little children will one day live in a nation where they will not be judged by the color of their skin, but by the content of their character. [3]

Examples

Example 4: Figuring Out What You've Been Asked to Do

Let's try and illustrate all of the preceding with an example. Let's assume your organization is expanding. You need more people and you've decided to run a job advertisement. This process seems straightforward enough: Write the ad, run it, and deal with the fallout from it. Let's see if applying our tools adds any value or provides us with any new insights.

Let's first try to understand what we're trying to do. How will we know when we're finished? This is actually a very interesting question, and the answer is not at all as obvious as would first appear. Are we finished when the ad runs? When we've processed the results? Run the interviews? Hired the people? Something else? In terms of the quality of what is delivered, if we spend large amounts of the company's money to run an ad, and we end up getting no responses, has this been a success? Do we care (on the basis that it's not our money)? If our existing people see an ad, will there be issues about salary scales or job descriptions or conditions? If the hiring of the people lies within the scope of what we are doing, then we will have to involve other people—the human resources department, at the very least. I hope you can see that even by asking only a few of our questions, we find that this business of running an ad is not at all as one-dimensional and well-defined as it might have appeared at first glance.

Now let's assume we make some decisions. We assume that running the ad will mean precisely that. It will encompass just the business of getting the ad into a particular newspaper. Anything else—processing the results, arranging and carrying out interviews, making job offers—will form part of a new little project. (Notice that this is completely arbitrary on our part; we could have chosen differently and still have been right.) So, we now know the answer to the question "What point in time constitutes its end point?" It's when the ad appears in the *Hamster and Furry Rodent Weekly* or wherever you're planning to run it.

What physical things will it produce? Well, it will produce the ad itself, in some form in which the newspaper can accept it. (Somebody's going to have to find out. Notice how this thought process begins to bridge us from the *what* we are trying to do to the *how* we will do it.) The quality? Because we've decided that the level of response to the ad is outside the scope of what we're doing here, the quality is going to be measured purely by the fact that the ad represents our company well. Thus we can identify some measures such as that it appears in a prominent part of the newspaper, that it sends out a good message about the company, that it contains no typos or misprints, and so on. (Reviews and proofreading will be required. Notice again the bridge from the what to the how.)

Finally, in terms of people issues, we decide to make sure that anything that appears in the ad is in the public domain within the company. In other words, nobody who already works in our company should be taken by surprise by the ad or find out things for the first time in it.

So, in summary, this venture involves running an ad that reflects well on the company and doesn't upset anyone already in the company. We are finished when such an ad has run successfully in the chosen newspaper.

Now let's move on to establishing whether this is what everyone wants. First, who is everyone? Well, let's list them:

- Us.

- Our boss—Imagine him or her opening the paper and reading an ad that he or she, for whatever reason, turned out to be unhappy with. Our boss can perhaps act as a proxy for all other higher-ups—bigger bosses, shareholders, and so on.

- Our existing employees.

- Potential employees.

- Our customers—We didn't start out expecting to see these people here, but it's true: Existing and potential customers will read the ad, so it must say something to them.

Do all these parties have win conditions? They sure do. They are listed in Table 2.1.

Table 2.1 Win conditions of the stakeholders.

Stakeholder	Win Conditions
Us	Run ad that reflects well on the company and doesn't upset anybody. It also should communicate why the jobs on offer are so attractive that you'd be mad not to apply.
Our boss	The ad sends out a positive message about the company.
Existing employees	Doesn't upset anybody—uses only material that is in the public domain. Sends out a message that the company is one that people want to work for.
Potential employees	Sends out a message that the company is one that people want to work for.
Our customers	Sends out a message that the company is expanding and is a good company to do business with.

I think you'll agree that this gives us a lot more insight into the nature of the ad we will write.

Finally, over the duration that this little project runs, nothing might change, or we could decide to run it in other newspapers, or include other jobs in the ad as well as those in our department, or any number of other changes. We need to be alert to these over the life of the project.

Example 5: Meetings (Part 1)

Here's another example of knowing what you're trying to do. Survey after survey affirms that most managers consider meetings to be the single biggest waste of their time [4]. I have a friend who writes the minutes of meetings *before* the meeting, and she has done this for years. In doing this, she focuses very clearly on the result she is trying to get from the meeting. She is saying, "Here's how I will know when this meeting has achieved its objectives."

This idea of the result you are trying to achieve is an idea that can be extended to all sorts of things:

- Presentations.

- Customer visits or sales calls.

- Project status reports. Write them *before* the period to which they are going to refer. Will having it in front of you keep you focused?

- The day ahead of you.

Example 6: Setting Goals

The visualization tool that we spoke of earlier is probably the best way I know to go about setting goals, be they business or personal ones. This notion is not a new idea. Nearly 500 years ago, Pope Leo X complained about Leonardo da Vinci [5]: "Here is a man, alas, who will never do anything, since he is thinking of the completion of his painting before he has started." This idea of thinking about the end is also enshrined in one of Stephen Covey's *The 7 Habits of Highly Effective People* [6]. Habit 2 is "Begin with the end in mind." Visualization is a great way of doing precisely that.

In a sense, we are all familiar with visualization. If we've ever daydreamed, then we've been engaging in visualization. In daydreams we run little movie clips in our heads in which we see ourselves doing things we really want to do. The best way to start setting personal goals is to picture what life will be like when that particular goal is achieved. Here are the kind of questions you could ask yourself to get the day-dream (or movie clip) rolling:

- There will come a day when this goal has been achieved. What will life be like then?

- How will you feel?

- What will your ambitions, hopes, and dreams be on that day?

- Will your standard of living have changed? If it is a business goal, will your position within the organization have changed?

- Will you have power, capabilities, or other assets that you don't have at the moment?

- How will you spend your days?

- What will a typical day be like? What will your routine be? Your schedule? Think through such a day from getting up in the morning to going to bed at night. Whom will you meet? Where will you eat your meals? What will you do (i.e., how will you occupy your time)? Will this make you happy?

- Are there other people who will be affected by this goal? Who are they? (From a business point of view, think about bosses, peers, customers, subordinates, team members, and other parts of the organization. From a personal point of view, there are family, friends, and acquaintances.)

- How will these other people be affected by the goal? What will reaching this goal mean to each of them?

- Why do you want to achieve this goal?

- Do the other people who will be affected by the goal have motivations with regard to the goal? Are these positive, neutral, or negative motivations?

- What will other people be saying about you—both the people who were affected by the goal and those who weren't affected, but who know you?

- What recognition, if any, are you hoping to achieve in achieving this goal?

- Will your view of yourself have changed? If so, how?

- Will you have changed as a person? If so, how?

- Do you think it is a difficult task you have set for yourself?

- Could it fail?

- How would you feel then? What would you do?

- What would you like to do after this goal is achieved?

- What would be the best possible outcome to this venture?

Example 7: Looking for Simple Causes

This example combines what we have learned in Principles 1 ("Many things are simple") and 2 ("Know what you're trying to do"). One of the things we do at my company is project rescues. A few years ago I was asked to do one for a large, complex project that was adrift from both a budgetary and elapsed time point of view. When I say the project was large, there were bits of it being done in a dozen countries. When I say it was complex, its purpose was to develop a very sophisticated software product.

The first day I arrived on the scene, the project manager handed me six large folders, each about three inches thick, and each bulging with paper. "You'll need to read these by way of background," he said. Trying to conceal my dismay, I asked if he could tell me the story of the project instead. Principle 2 tells us that one possible reason the undertaking could have gotten into trouble is because the project's goal hadn't been clearly defined. Maybe this was the case here. If not, then maybe I would have to begin reading the reams of paper.

As it turned out, the goal of the project hadn't been properly defined. Six months into the project, the requirements and high-level design were to have been completed and agreed on so that software development could start. Not only were they not agreed on; they were only partially written. Without going any further, we had unearthed the main reason why the project had run into trouble.

As a footnote to this story, I once bid for another piece of project rescue business. I reckoned that in bidding five days of my time plus expenses I would get the job done, come up with all the answers, get the report written, have a bit of contingency, and make some profit. I didn't get the job. Subsequently I learned it had gone to a big consulting company that had put a consultant in for two months. The theory seemed to be that complex projects required complex reasons for them to go wrong. This has *never* been my experience.

So What Should You Do?

1. Keep a list of the things you're trying to do—your "projects."

2. Use the tools described in the "Tools" section of this chapter to analyze new things as they come along, before adding them to your list of projects.

3. Check your list of projects regularly—ideally every day, and in the worst case, every week—to see whether changes have occurred to the goals of your projects. If so, you need to rerun the maximize-the-win-conditions-of-the-stakeholders analysis.

PRINCIPLE 1: MANY THINGS ARE SIMPLE

PRINCIPLE 2: KNOW WHAT YOU'RE TRYING TO DO

References

1. Carroll, Lewis, *The Complete Works of Lewis Carroll*, London: Penguin, 1988, p. 64.

2. Boehm, Barry W. and Ross, Rony, "Theory-W Software Project Management: Principles and Examples," *IEEE Transactions on Software Engineering*, Vol. 15, No.7, July 1989, pp. 902–916.

3. Hampton, Henry and Freyer, Steve, *Voices of Freedom*, New York: Bantam, 1990, p. 167.

4. Schrage, Michael, "The Broadband Promise: Every E-Mail a Spielberg Epic," *Fortune*, Fall 2000, Special Issue.

5. White, Michael, *Leonardo*, London: Abacus, 2001, p. 388.

6. Covey, Stephen R., *The 7 Habits of Highly Effective People*, London: Simon & Schuster, 1999, p. 96.

3

THERE IS ALWAYS A SEQUENCE OF EVENTS

This chapter shows that to do anything requires a sequence of events. Knowing this gives you the skills to plan, prioritize, accelerate projects, and get many things done at the same time. It also shows why "firefighting" can become the exception rather than the rule.

Questions

1. In keeping your inbox to manageable proportions, which of the following is the best strategy?

   (a) Clear it every day.

   (b) Let it pile up. The important things will always float to the surface somehow, so once a month throw it all in the garbage.

   (c) Go through it every day, deal only with those things that align with your priorities, and once a month throw it all in the garbage.

   (d) Go through it every day, deal only with those things that align with your priorities, and once a week deal with all of the other stuff.

2. You're planning a project. Your business is high-tech (i.e., it's not construction or manufacturing or something like that). The conventional wisdom has it that you can only plan in great detail for the next phase of the project and after that it's all pretty much guesswork. With regard to this statement, do you:

   (a) Agree?

   (b) Disagree?

   (c) Not see how it can be any other way?

   (d) Possibly disagree, but feel that the effort involved in building lots of detail would—by orders of magnitude—outweigh the benefit?

3. You must write a report and deliver it to a client. Your boss must write a key part of the report. It's only a page, but she's notorious for procrastinating on such things. What do you do?

   (a) Wait until she delivers and tell the customer that she's to blame ("It's been on my boss's desk for weeks now").

   (b) Write it yourself and send it out without telling her.

(c) Write a fill-in-the-blanks version. Then talk your boss through it, fill in the blanks, and send it out.

(d) Send the report out minus your boss's bit.

Answers

1. **(a) 0 points**

I dithered on whether to give you a point here, but I think this is a bad idea. You'll spend too much valuable time dealing with trivia.

(b) 1 point

You get a well-deserved point here. I love your bravado, your self-confidence, your devil-may-care attitude, and your daring. However, sooner or later you'll get yourself into trouble doing things like this (even if your inbox is always empty).

(c) 5 points

This is my favorite. Get the important things done, and consign the rest to the garbage where it truly belongs.

(d) 4 points

You get most of the points for this, but I still think the previous answer is better.

2. **(a) 0 points**

It might be the conventional wisdom, but I can tell you from experience, it isn't right.

(b) 5 points

Yup.

(c) 0 points

Read this chapter to see another way.

(d) 0 points

Nope—read this chapter.

3. **(a) 0 points**

I don't think so.

(b) 3 points

But this depends a lot on the sensitivity or otherwise of the report. Take 5 points here if you and your boss understand each other perfectly.

(c) 5 points

Why not? Your boss will love you for it, the customer's happy, and there's very little risk.

(d) 3 points

Same answer as (b).

Scores

15 points   That's a good result. Well done.

12–14 points   So is this.

Less than 12 points   No need to beat yourself up. These are tricky questions.

The Idea

A few years ago, two people I know decided to take their children to Disneyland. They were staying in Santa Monica, California, at the time. They explained their plan to me: Leave Santa Monica after breakfast and drive to Disneyland, spend the day there, visit all the good rides, come back, put the children to bed with a babysitter, have a bath to wind down, dress up, go out, and have a nice relaxing dinner.

My immediate reaction was, "That's gonna be one long day." I guess it's the project manager in me, but it sounded to me like that

Saturday wouldn't come to a close until well into Sunday. When I mentally strung all the tasks together, there seemed to be too much going on there. When I did it on paper, my suspicions were confirmed. Here's the best-case scenario of what their Saturday was going to look like:

Depart Santa Monica	9:00 a.m.	With kids in tow, you'll be doing well if you achieve this!
Santa Monica to Disneyland	9:00–11:00 a.m.	
A day at Disneyland	11:00 a.m.–7:00 p.m.	This has to be a minimum of eight hours.
Disneyland to Santa Monica	7:00–9:00 p.m.	
Kids to bed	9:00–11:00 p.m	You can't just rush them off to bed when you get back.
Bath to wind down	11:00 p.m–12:00 a.m.	This has to be at least an hour to get the value of it at all.
Dress up	12:00–1:00 a.m.	It's now Sunday.
Find and get to restaurant	1:00–1:30 a.m.	Assuming there's one that's open in the middle of the night!
Nice relaxing dinner	1:30–4:30 a.m.	Say three hours. At this stage, the diners will have been up for close to 24 hours! Relaxed? I'd say they'd be comatose!

The point of this story is not to show that anyone was stupid. The point is that there is always a sequence of events, and many people either don't realize this, or, if they do, they don't seem to understand the implications of the sequence of events.

For some reason—I think it's something I got from my father—I'm very precise and, I guess, old-fashioned about time. If I tell somebody I'll meet them at 3 p.m., I'll be there before that. If they're not there at 3 p.m., I'll very quickly begin to assume there's a problem. It's taken me a long time to realize that very few people are like me in this respect. The difference, I've come to believe, is that very few people think in terms of a sequence of events.

Somebody agrees to meet you at a specific time. In general, in my experience, that person doesn't take into account other meetings, things running late, getting across town, finding an unfamiliar place, or finding parking, all things that can blow the appointment with you completely out of the water. I once worked at a company where people would wander into a meeting, say on a Wednesday, and ask, "Is this the Monday marketing meeting?" This was my sequence-of-events theory gone mad.

Sequences of events are so important because—quite simply—without them, nothing gets done. Let's say you're buying a house and the real estate agent calls you and says, "The owners of the house like your offer—it looks like we have a deal on our hands." "Great," you say. "Yeah, it is great," he says, and the call finishes. Now, if that is all that happens, nothing will get done. Because the real estate agent is waiting for you to make the next move, and you think his is the next move, a standoff ensues. If, however, you ask, "So what happens next?" or he volunteers, "So, here's what has to happen now," then this is the cue for you and the agent to build a sequence of events.

Maybe you would never let this happen if you were buying a house or engaged in some other important personal event, but how many times have you gone to a meeting where the following has happened? There is a complete meeting of minds. Everybody agrees that the issue needs to be resolved and the way forward is agreed on. Then everyone files out of the room and—surprise, surprise—nothing gets done because no sequence of events gets built; or worse still, because nobody summarizes (ideally in writing) the actions arising from the meeting, everybody builds his or her own version of the sequence of events.

In her book *The Seven Deadly Sins of Business* [1], Eileen Shapiro discusses the reasons that companies get into trouble. The first "deadly sin" is that too many companies identify an aggressive goal, vision, or target and then pay scant attention to how that goal, vision, or target will be achieved. She is saying precisely what I am saying: If there is no sequence of events, nothing gets done.

A different way of thinking about all of this is to say that sequences of events are your best shot at understanding what will happen in the future. This is just a complicated way of saying that sequences of events are *plans*, or to be more slightly more precise, sequences of events are the foundations of plans. Good sequences of events are the foundations of good plans. How was some great undertaking like D-Day planned? Primarily because many people built large, complicated, interconnected sequences of events [2].

If you know what you are trying to do (see Chapter 2) and can build sequences of events to do it, then you are well on your way to accomplishing the things you want to do. The next question then is, what tools are there that can help you to build sequences of events? It turns out there are seven of them:

1. Make the journey in your head.

2. Do it in as much detail as possible.

3. Use knowledge and assumptions.

4. Count the bricks in the wall.

5. There always has to be another way.

6. Record what actually happens.

7. Look for connections.

I discuss them each in turn in the next section.

Tools

Make the Journey in Your Head

When people were planning D-Day, it is likely that nobody said, "Let's just send five divisions over there and see how they get on." Instead the planners tried to think through how they would get from their current situation to the goal they had identified. They imagined, speculated on, and wrote down the sequence of events that would take them forward: the cause and effect, how each event or job would lead to the next one until eventually, strung in a long chain, the events (or jobs) led from the starting point to the destination. (I often use the word *job* here as it is a well-understood word, and has a healthy sense of work ethic about it!)

Do It in as Much Detail as Possible

The next important thing to bear in mind is the level of detail in which the sequence of events was described. The D-Day people didn't just say this:

1. Start.

2. Rustle up five divisions.

3. Ship them to Normandy.

4. Have them get ashore.

5. The end.

Although at its highest level of abstraction the plan might have indeed looked like this, for it to have been in any way valid or usable, it needed to be worked down to as much detail as could possibly be imagined. The devil is in the details, the old saying goes, and how true it is. It is only when we burrow down into the details, imagining (making the journey in our heads) the various events taking place, and how the result of one event is then the starting point for the next event, that we can unearth all the potential obstacles that lie ahead. For my money, in most of the situations we encounter these days, a level of detail (or breakdown) where every job can be measured in the range of one to five person-days is what you need to aim for.

Use Knowledge and Assumptions

Of course, you might object and say, "But I can't know all the events, I can't know all the details." This is indeed true. So then the rule is simple: Where you have knowledge, use it. Where you don't, where—in the course of your mental journey—you come up against something and you have no idea what comes next, then you make some assumption. For example, how did the Allies know what kind of opposition they would face on Omaha Beach? They didn't, for sure, but they had some knowledge, based on intelligence, reconnaissance, and so on. For the rest they made assumptions that enabled them to continue to chain an unbroken sequence of events together.

Count the Bricks in the Wall

Finally, don't forget that things might have to be done more than once. You might be involved, for example, in something that has to take place at several of your company's sites. In that case, once you've identified the sequence of events once, you can essentially duplicate it for the other situations. This tool is about knowing how much has to be done.

There Always Has to be Another Way

There's more than one way to skin a cat, the saying goes. This tool says that there is always more than one possible sequence of events. Once you've figured out what you're trying to do (Principle 2, "Know what you're trying to do"), there are endless ways of getting there. In keeping with Principle 1 ("Many things are simple"), we will always be looking for the simpler ways to do things, but this tool is also about determination and never giving up looking for ways to do things.

Brainstorming is a powerful way of doing this. At the risk of telling you things you already know, do it in two passes. First of all, try to come up with as many ways as you can think of to solve the particular problem. Every idea is allowed at this stage. No idea, whether possible or impossible, wacky or sensible, vastly expensive or free, realistic or unrealistic, civilized or uncivilized, is ruled out. Write them all down on, say, a flipchart page, then go back over the list and select those that meet certain criteria that you set.

Record What Actually Happens

All of the previous tools assumed you were starting from a blank sheet of paper. Often this is the case: The particular thing you are doing has not been done before and you are setting off into the great unknown. More often, though, we are doing things that have been done before. The planners of D-Day, for example, learned many lessons from the disastrous amphibious raid on Dieppe two years earlier. It should thus be possible to draw on other people's experience to build the sequence of events. Our team, our peers, or somebody somewhere in the organization might know something. Even if that is not the case, that shouldn't stop you from quickly building up your own bank of knowledge as your own venture unfolds. Figure 3.1 shows a form for doing precisely that.

In the leftmost column, write down the major events, phases, or jobs that took place in your undertaking. They might be things like requirements gathering, design, planning, and so on. Then there are three sets of four columns. The three sets are for (a) what you planned, (b) what actually happened, and (c) the difference between the two. The blocks of four columns enable you to enter the following:

- The elapsed time for that particular phase (planned, actual, and the difference between the two).

PHASE	PLANNED						ACTUAL						DIFFERENCE					
	Elapsed (days)	%	Work (person-days)	%			Elapsed (days)	%	Work (person-days)	%			Elapsed (days)	%	Work (person-days)	%		

Figure 3.1   A form for building up your bank of knowledge.

- The elapsed time as a percentage of the overall elapsed time. (You calculate this when the project is over and you know what the final elapsed time was.) Again you do planned, actual, and the difference.

- The amount of work that went into each phase (planned, actual, and differences).

- The work in each phase as a percentage of the overall amount of work in the project. (Again, you calculate this when the project is over and the final amount of work is known.) There are planned, actual, and difference values as before.

An example of a completed form is shown in Figure 3.2.

The material captured in this way is like treasure. This statement is true even if you are at the beginning of your data-gathering career and have only one completed project in your databank. The next time you need to plan something even remotely similar, you will find that you are able to get useful information from your databank. In addition, if you are asked to review other people's plans, you can again compare what they are proposing with what is in your databank, and—almost always—draw useful conclusions.

Look for Connections

Leonardo da Vinci was only one of the world's thinkers who made the observation that everything is connected to everything else. The theme recurs again and again in his writing. Here is just one example: "Every part is disposed to unite with the whole, that it may thereby escape from its own incompleteness" [3]. In generating sequences of events, one of the most useful things you can do is to look for connections between the sequences. Such connections might enable you to move several things along at once or accelerate one sequence by carrying out an activity in another.

PHASE	PLANNED				ACTUAL				DIFFERENCE			
	Elapsed (days)	% (2)	Work (person-days)	% (3)	Elapsed (days)	% (5)	Work (person-days)	% (3)	Elapsed (days)	% (2)	Work (person-days)	% (3)
Requirements	40	26	27	4	15	14	34	6	-25	-63	7	26
Design (Prototype)	14	9	22	4	15	14	33	6	1	7	11	50
Coding	32	21	184	30	53	48	164	30	21	66	-20	-11
System Test (4)	60	39	115	19	47	43	159	29	-13	-22	44	38
Technical Writing	84	55	99	16	88	80	88	16	4	5	-11	-11
Contingency	14	9	103	17	0	0	0	0	-14	-100	-103	-100
Project Management	140	91	46	8	110	100	56	10	-30	-21	9	20
Totals	(1)	(1)	596	98	(1)	(1)	533	96			-63	

Notes:
(1) Adding these doesn't necessarily make sense because some of the phases of the project overlapped.
(2) As a percentage of the total elapsed time (i.e., 154 days).
(3) As a percentage of the total work (i.e., 610 person-days).
(4) Estimated elapsed includes both writing the tests and carrying them out. Effort includes this plus bug fixing.
(5) As a percentage of the total elapsed time (i.e., 110 days).
(6) As a percentage of the total actual work (i.e., 554 person-days).

Figure 3.2   A completed project knowledge form.

These then, are the seven tools that enable us to build sequences of events. It has to be said that many people never go through the trouble of building sequences of events. They feel it is too much effort (it isn't), they feel that they can't (they can), or they feel that the effort far outweighs the benefit (not true either). For these people, the term *firefighting* has been coined. Firefighting is the situation in which some unexpected thing happens and effort—sometimes enormous effort—has to be put into sorting it out.

Don't get me wrong: Sometimes unexpected things do happen and there are real firefights. However, many firefights need never have occurred if only people had exercised their gray matter and gone through the trouble of building sequences of events.

Finally, just as a footnote, if your business is project management, you'll probably have deduced by now that a sequence of events is remarkably similar to what you would call a work breakdown structure (WBS).

Examples

Example 8: Estimating

It might be that one of the things you have to do in your job is that exciting blood sport known as *estimating*. I call it a blood sport because, in estimating, you have to be able to predict the future. How successfully you do this will, more or less, determine your career progression and success. In the past I have taught estimating, and one of the things I often did during those classes was hold up a schedule (which was based on estimates) in one hand and a lottery ticket in the other and ask the class, "What do these have in common?" (Somebody once muttered, "If I won the lottery I wouldn't have to do any more of these stupid schedules!") What they have in common is that they are both predictions of the future. We'd all like to feel that when we produce an estimate, the odds of it happening are better than those of picking a winning lottery ticket. (Although, I've definitely seen estimates where the smart money would have been on the lottery ticket!)

The tools just described are the things you need to help you build accurate, resilient estimates. In general, when estimating, people are concerned with three things:

- How long will something take? (What is its duration or elapsed time?)

- How much work is involved in something? (Work is sometimes referred to as *effort*.)

- How much will something cost? (What is its budget?)

Notice, too, that duration and work are not the same. Duration is how long something will take; work is how much effort is involved in that particular thing. For instance, an hour-long meeting involving six people has a duration of one hour, but an effort (work) of six person-hours. In my experience, confusion between these two quantities is a source of much great human unhappiness. Imagine, for example, your boss comes in, flips a report onto your desk, and asks, "How long would it take you to look at that?" You look at it, think for a moment and reply, "Oh, about an hour." Now if you've given effort but your boss thought he got duration, can you see the potential for unhappiness? Your boss thinks he's going to get your comments back within the hour. You know—looking at the current backlog you have (300 unread e-mails, for example)—that it will be weeks before you can get to his document.

I've seen all sort of scientific and pseudo-scientific ways of estimating in different disciplines. If you're in the software field, see Barry Boehm's *Software Engineering Economics* [4], which contains a comprehensive treatment of it. However, for my money, nothing compares with the following description of estimating—a description that ends up defining both the process of estimating and the finished product of that process. It's taken from the book *My Indecision Is Final* [5], and describes the preparations that had to be made by Sir Richard Attenborough prior to shooting his movie, *Gandhi*:

> He [Attenborough] had to shoot the film during the cool season in India, starting in November and finishing the following April or May. (The summer would simply be too hot: a film crew could not function in 110 degree heat.) But to start in November he had to make preparations now, six months ahead: hiring the cast and crew, building the sets, sorting out the costumes, getting all the permissions needed to shoot in India, shipping the equipment and so on. The tasks, known as pre-production, are fairly straightforward if you are shooting in your own country, but are horrendously complicated when you are shooting overseas. To take a simple example, if you are going to fly in 125 people to make a movie, you have to book the hotel rooms and pay for them, or at least put down some sort of deposit, well in advance. *That means knowing now exactly where you will want each of those 125 people to be on any given day over the four or six months that the film will be shooting.* [Italics added.]

So, if you are charged with estimating, this is what you must do. Establish, using the tools described earlier in this chapter, what everyone is doing every day of the venture. (In Chapter 4, I describe a tool known as a *strip board* that is used in the movie industry to do precisely this.) It then becomes very straightforward matter to estimate the following:

- How long

- How much work

- How much money

Figure 3.3 shows an example of estimating work and using assumptions (contained in the field headed Notes).

ID	Task Name	Work (in days)	Predecessor	Notes
1	1 The Project	44		
2	1.1 START	0		
3	1.2 Project plan and scope meeting	9	2	9 people for 1 day
4	1.3 Produce requirements document	27	3	
5	1.3.1 Research user requirements	7		
6	1.3.1.1 Get info on competitive prods	0.5		Charlie'll do it
7	1.3.1.2 Review with marketing	2 6		Assume 3 market. people and Charlie @ ½ day each gives 2 days work
8	1.3.1.3 Identify users	0.5	7	Marketing guy—his estimate
9	1.3.1.4 Prepare user questionnaires	2	8	Charlie says he'll do it. Take him a couple of days
10	1.3.1.5 Distribute questionnaires	0.5	9	Admin. person. On the basis that ½ day is the smallest unit possible
11	1.3.1.6 Retrieve questionnaires	0.5	10FS+1wk	½ day's work chasing. Probably 5 days elapsed time to get it done
12	1.3.1.7 Analyze information	1	11	Charlie and a marketing person @ 1/2 day each
13	1.3.2 Write requirements document	9	12	Charlie. Use company standard 9 section format @ 1 day per section
14	1.3.3 Review cycle	10.5	13	
15	1.3.3.1 Circulate	0.5		Admin. person. On the basis that ½ day is the smallest unit possible
16	1.3.3.2 Individual review	2.5	15	5 reviewers, ½ each, allow 1 week elapsed time in which to happen
17	1.3.3.3 Review meeting	3	16	Charlie and 5 reviewers @ ½ day each
18	1.3.3.4 Changes to document	2.5	17	Charlie—his estimate
19	1.3.3.5 Circulate again	0.5	18	Same as earlier, see "Circulate"
20	1.3.3.6 Second review	1.5	19	5 reviewers, 1–2 hrs each, do ASAP—give a deadline for comments
21	1.3.4 Signoff	0.5	14	Assuming no substantial changes. Admin person chases signoffs
22	1.3.5 Requirements complete	0	21	
23	1.4 Produce system/acceptance test plan	8	4	
24	1.4.1 Research	5		
25	1.4.2 Write navigation tests	3	24	
26	1.4.2.1 Define test sequence	1		
27	1.4.2.2 Write test scripts	1	26	
28	1.4.2.3 Define expected results	1	27	
29	1.4.3 Write functionality tests	0	25	

Figure 3.3   Estimating work and using assumptions.

From what is contained in Figure 3.3 it would be possible to work out elapsed times—provided we knew people's availability. In addition, if we knew labor rates it would be possible to work out what things cost. In the next chapter (in Figure 4.2), you will see estimates laid out a different way—on a strip board. Notice, too, that there's another example of estimating at the beginning of this chapter. We did it when we planned the Disneyland trip. It's all there—jobs, elapsed times, assumptions, who's doing what—the works.

Example 9: Meetings (Part 2)

Let's say, for example, you're going to a meeting. Are you just at the mercy of whatever pops up at the meeting or can you do a bit better than that? The question is rhetorical because, of course, you can do better than that. For starters, you can decide what result you want to get from the meeting (Principle 2) and then you can figure out how you might get it (Principle 3).

Let's say the meeting is with a client, and it's a difficult meeting. It's about rebuilding a relationship that's gone off the rails—not that anything particularly disastrous happened, but it was perhaps mishandled at times, incorrect perceptions were allowed to spring up and fester, and generally, the relationship wasn't given professional tender loving care.

So you start by asking, "What are we trying to get from the meeting?" An order? Hardly. Even if by some bizarre turn of fate they offered you one, you should almost (I said "almost"!) be thinking in terms of declining it. Your emphasis today is on rebuilding the relationship. On the basis that Rome wasn't built in a day, maybe you decide that the best you can hope to do today is to give them a feeling that you care. You want them to know, at the conclusion of the meeting, that you want to do business with them in the future and that you have value you think you can add to their business. However, you don't want it to be a sales pitch. Let's say there are two of you going—you, who have inherited the account, and your boss. You have asked for the meeting and they are giving you 20 minutes. (The detail is somewhat unimportant here except to illustrate things. What's important is how you have clearly set out what you do and don't hope to get from the meeting.)

Now comes the sequence of events. You discuss it with your boss beforehand and settle on something like the following:

1. Your boss will open the meeting. He will thank them for taking the time out of their busy days, and explain that the purpose is to begin the process of rebuilding something that has been neglected. He will explain how you think you can still add value and how you hope to be a valuable supplier to them in the future. Then he will give them an opening to have a gripe.

2. You assume they will take the opportunity and that this will be the greater part of the meeting.

3. You agree that you will take their gripes on the chin, not trying to give excuses or correct them even if they're wrong. You might occasionally tell them of steps you have taken and procedures you have put in place to fix some of the problems they describe. Your boss will lead and you'll take notes.

4. You decide you'll allow the first three items to take, at most, 15 minutes so that you have a few minutes to close and get out within the 20 minutes they gave you.

5. Because every meeting should end with some kind of action—to keep the chain of events unbroken—you might mention to them that you plan to bid for the next piece of business that comes out (action on you) or not to forget you next time they're looking for a supplier (action on them).

6. Finally, you'll thank them for their input, remind them of the value you can add, and reiterate that you want to put the past behind you and move forward into what will hopefully be a better relationship for both parties. Then you will say your goodbyes.

In terms of your goal, this should get you there. If it all goes horribly wrong, there's probably not much you can do except to get out with as much of your dignity intact as possible.

Again, the details are less important than the idea of using the two principles—figure out what you're trying to do and then put a sequence of events in place to do it.

Example 10: Dealing with Lots of Things and Prioritizing

You might be trying to do several things. If you haven't established a sequence of events for each one, then it's quite likely you'll end up skipping from one to the other, never sure (a) if things are progressing, and (b) if the right things are progressing.

Once you have a sequence of events for each of the things you're trying to do, then all of this changes. Then each sequence of events is like a stack of jobs to be done. By taking the top item from each stack, you move that particular task forward. If you take the top item from every stack, then everything gets moved forward. Even more usefully, when new things come winging in, you can check them against the stacks you're working on and see if they are relevant to things going on in the stacks. If they are, you should deal with them; if not, you can put them aside. Thus the best way to deal with an inbox is as follows: Screen it for anything that needs to be dealt with right away (i.e., anything that is relevant to one of the stacks you have in progress); otherwise, leave it in a pile to be cleared once a week or once a month—the longer the interval the better, in my view.

If, in addition to all of this you are good at prioritizing, then you can restrict the number of things you concentrate on (and hence the number of stacks you have on the go) to the bare minimum that will make the biggest difference. (One suspects an 80/20 rule is operating here—do 20 percent of the things and get 80 percent of your job done.) To be good at prioritizing, just do the following: Look at all the things you have going and ask yourself, "If I could only do one of these things, which would it be?" Having answered it, take the remaining items and ask the question again. Do this until all items have been assigned a priority. Try to ensure that two items don't have the same priority, because then they're not really prioritized, are they?

Finally, as pointed out earlier, having sequences of events for each of the things you're trying to do means that you can look for connections between things. Something that you plan to do for project A might also affect project B. Then you should be very eager to do it and it should shoot right to the top of your priority list. Conversely, if accomplishing something from stack A will have a negative effect on something else, you might want to analyze it a bit more carefully before preceding.

Example 11: Speeding Things Up

Having sequences of events for each of the things you are trying to do also means that you can accelerate them. You know how it goes: There's something you're trying to do, and it invariably involves other people. You do your bit, give it to them, and there it often hangs in some form of suspended animation.

However, if you have a stack of events, you can look further down the stack rather than just at the top item and see other things that could be done to move the project forward. Thus, while you're waiting for the other thing to happen, you can still make progress. Often this has the nice side effect of putting pressure on the laggards to complete their work.

Example 12: Dealing with Specialists

Doctors, lawyers, and IT people are probably the worst offenders, though many of us do it. You know the kind of thing I mean—somebody takes the attitude that they know better than you and that you should just leave things to them. They talk (often condescendingly) to you in the techno-babble of their particular discipline in the hope that it will baffle you into silence. If that doesn't work, and you actually question them, they continue to send waves of techno-babble to intimidate you. Almost always—particularly with lawyers and IT people—there's a sense that "it'll take as long as it takes. Don't ask why—it just will."

The truth is that doctors, lawyers, and IT people—indeed, all specialists—are as subject to the principle of sequences of events as the next person. With doctors, to hand your health or even your life over to someone like this is crazy. With lawyers, it is often your financial well-being that is at stake. And many of us these days know the frustrations of dealing with IT people. If you are in charge—which you are if you hire a doctor, hire a lawyer, or manage an IT person—then, among other things, the onus is on *them* to tell *you* clearly and unambiguously what the sequence of events is. Furthermore, you are entitled to question the sequence of events. This is particularly true of lawyers and IT people: What happens next? What does what you just said mean? What does it translate into in simple language? Who is doing what? Why does it take this long? ("It just does" is not a good enough answer.) Why can't it be done quicker? What's the hold up? Explain to me in simple language who is doing what. What am I expected to do? Keep doing this until you get a clear picture in your mind of what is going on. Don't be afraid to make suggestions or offer improvements to the plan (i.e., the sequence of events). Once they get the hang of how the game is going to be played, they'll deliver a much better service for your (or your company's) money.

Example 13: Problem Solving

We can use the three principles we've seen so far to come up with a method for problem solving. The first thing we need to know is what exactly the problem is. Principle 2, "Know what you're trying to do," reiterates this. Sometimes, the stated issue is not the real issue; sometimes, people phrase a problem by stating a solution; sometimes, even if a problem is stated correctly, by pulling back and seeing the bigger picture, you can solve the problem more completely. The "understand what you're trying to do" tool (discussed in Chapter 2) enables you to state the problem clearly.

Having identified the problem, it's useful to know what the ideal solution would be. Among other things, this enables you to gauge the quality of any other solutions that emerge. The "know if what you're trying to do is what everyone wants" tool (discussed in Chapter 2) is a way of figuring out the solution that would best meet the needs of all of the parties involved in the problem.

You know what problem you're trying to solve, and you know what the ideal solution would be. Now, let's identify a range of possible solutions. Principle 3, "There is always a sequence of events," enables us to do this. In particular, the "there always has to be another way" tool enables you to find other solutions to the problem.

Finally, knowing the ideal solution, pick from your range of possible solutions the one that comes closest to the ideal.

Example 14: Discussions That Lead Nowhere

Have you ever had one of those discussions that leads nowhere? I'm sure you know the kind of thing I mean. You and a colleague (or maybe several of them) have a discussion in which you are entirely in agreement about something. That somebody really should do something seems to be the unspoken subtext. However, at the end of the discussion, everyone walks away and nothing happens. (Actually, in my experience, whole meetings have often been conducted like this.)

Knowing that there is always a sequence of events can prevent this from happening. If there is agreement on an issue, then for anything to happen, a sequence of events must flow from that agreement. Pointing this out and putting even one or two jobs in motion (i.e., putting actions on people) ensures that whatever great idea was hatched during the discussion is not forgotten, but rather is acted on.

So What Should You Do?

1. Keep a list of the things you're trying to do.

2. Update it regularly—every day, every week, or whatever schedule works for you.

3. Use Principle 2 to understand new things as they come along. Then use the tools described in the "Tools" section of this chapter to build sequences of events. Keep the sequences of events in stacks and work the stacks as described.

4. Always look for action lists after meetings, phone calls, and so on.

5. Always try to have a plan (sequence of events)—for a meeting, for a working day, or for a project. Things will go so much more smoothly as a result.

6. Use brainstorming to generate alternate ways forward and, hence, sequences of events.

7. Make bread in parallel with doing something else. Bread making is a classic example of a sequence of events. Making bread while doing one or more other things is a great way of practicing doing many things at once (i.e., managing sequences of events).

PRINCIPLE 1: MANY THINGS ARE SIMPLE

PRINCIPLE 2: KNOW WHAT YOU'RE TRYING TO DO

PRINCIPLE 3: THERE IS ALWAYS A SEQUENCE OF EVENTS

References

1. Shapiro, Eileen, *The Seven Deadly Sins of Business*, Oxford, England: Capstone, 1998.

2. Nalty, Bernard C. and Prichard, Russell A., *D-Day: 'Operation Overlord' From Its Planning to the Liberation of Paris*, London: Salamander Books, 1999.

3. Gelb, Michael, *How to Think Like Leonardo Da Vinci*, London: Thorsons, 1998, p. 221.

4. Boehm, Barry, *Software Engineering Economics*, Englewood Cliffs, NJ: Prentice Hall, 1981.

5. Eberts, Jake and Ilott, Terry, *My Indecision Is Final*, Berkeley, CA: Atlantic Monthly Press, 1990, p. 257.

4

THINGS DON'T GET DONE IF PEOPLE DON'T DO THEM

This chapter makes the rather obvious point that things won't be done if people don't do them. In particular, things won't get done if people don't have the time to do them.

Questions

1. You're involved in a rescue of a project or venture. In other words, it's all gone horribly wrong and you've been called in to clean up the mess. You discover there is a plan—and the plan is actually current (i.e., it has been recently updated). The plan has a well-defined goal, which has stayed relatively stable, and what looks like a comprehensive list of jobs (sequence of events). In looking at the plan you find that many of the jobs—particularly those that were meant to finish a long time ago—have phrases like "New hire," "TBD," and "A N Other" against them (i.e., generic names rather than real people's names).

   (a) Is this the main reason why the venture went wrong?

   (b) Is it something else?

   (c) Is it too soon to say—must you go and gather more information about the status of the project?

   (d) Is it nothing to do with the project, but rather with technical issues involved in the venture?

2. John shows up from central casting to work for you. He says he's available "full time." If this is true (i.e., if he genuinely has no other things to work on), and you discount vacation and holidays, how many real days of his time are you getting in a working week?

   (a) 3.75 days

   (b) Closer to (but greater than) 4 days

   (c) 2.5 days

   (d) Nearly 5 days

3. You're ready to begin a new venture with the merry band of brothers and sisters that you've either chosen, inherited, or otherwise acquired. Of the following, which is most likely to sink your venture?

   (a) Poor salaries.

(b) Poor working conditions.

(c) Not playing to people's strengths.

(d) Poor management by you.

Answers

1. (a) 5 points

If the goal was stable (Principle 2) and the sequence of events was well thought out (Principle 3), then you can depend on it. Stands to reason, doesn't it? If things were meant to be done and they weren't, then of course, it's going to go wrong.

(b) 2 points

There might be other considerations, but I think you'll find that with a good goal and a good sequence of events, this is almost certainly the prime contributor.

(c) 1 point

You can go gather more data, but I'd be surprised if it materially changed your initial findings.

(d) 1 point

Again, it's a possibility, but in my experience, it is rarely the cause of the problem if the other conditions that I've described are present.

2. (a) 5 points

It could well be—especially if his time management isn't the tightest.

(b) 5 points

This is the best you're going to get. With the best time management in the world, he's going to lose more than an hour a day.

(c) 5 points

You might argue—validly—that it depends on John.

(d) 0 points

Definitely not.

3. (a) 1 point

Most likely? It won't help, but I don't think so.

(b) 0 points

Not at all.

(c) 5 points

Yes. Play to people's weakness and it'll go down the tubes faster than you can say "human resources issue."

(d) 3 points

It's not most likely, but it's a close second to (c).

Scores

15 points   Although the scores in the second question increased your chances of getting a 15, I think you still did well here.

10–14 points   Nothing wrong with this. You've got a good sense of the infinite capacity of people to surprise.

Less than 10 points   As in the last chapter, these are also tricky questions.

The Idea

Once you've figured out what it is you're trying to do (Principle 2, "Know what you're trying to do") and what needs to happen to get it done (Principle 3, "There is always a sequence of events"), the next step is to get the things done. That is what this chapter is all about.

A couple of years ago, my ex-wife's nephew spent a few weeks in our company on a work experience from school. Shortly after he started with us, I was chatting with him and he asked, "What exactly do you do here?" I explained that we were a project management company. We sold our services to high-tech and knowledge industries. We did training, consulting, and ran projects for clients. He asked about the training course: "What kinds of things do you teach them?" "Oh," I said, "for example, we teach that if you have a big job to do, you break it up into lots of smaller jobs." He seemed happy enough with that for openers. "So what else?" he asked. "Well, we teach them that jobs don't get done if people don't do them." At this he smiled. "Do you charge a lot for this?" he asked. "It's not cheap," I replied. His smile broadened and he began to shake his head. "I'd better go back to work," he said.

It's so sickeningly obvious, and yet jobs *don't* get done if people don't do them and if enough jobs don't get done, then things go awry, sometimes badly. In general, people don't maliciously set out not to do things, but there are a variety of reasons why it can happen. The most obvious ones are these:

- Confusion—They didn't know they were meant to do something or precisely what it was they were meant to do.

- Overcommitment—They knew they were meant to do it but they didn't have the time available.

- Inability—They didn't have the expertise, experience, or training to do the job.

If we are to address the problem of people not doing certain things, our tools must tackle these three problems. The following tools are introduced in the "Tools" section of this chapter:

- Make sure every job has somebody to do it. This should deal with individual confusion.

- Dance cards, to deal, first of all, with overcommitment, but also with confusion within an organization.

- Maximizing the strengths of the team. This should deal with inability.

- The strip board that will tackle all three in one fell swoop!

Tools

Make Sure Every Job Has Somebody to Do It

Our first tool is a pretty straightforward one. We just want to make sure that at the end of a meeting, after a phone call, or at the start of a project or venture that we know who has to do what. At the beginning of a venture, you sometimes might not know who's going to work on what. They might not have been identified, assigned, or hired. In such a case, it is perfectly valid for you to have certain jobs in your sequences of events in which nobody has been identified to do it. Then it is fine if you put in generic names like Marketing Person, Engineer, Designer, or even the dreaded TBDs or New Hires.

However, some time *before* that event is due to happen, there had better be a warm, living, loving human being in place who is actually going to get the job done.

Dance Cards

You might not have necessarily thought of things in this way before, but much of life is a problem in supply and demand. We don't have enough money (supply) to do all the things we'd like to do (demand). Or we have a business and it is successful—revenue (supply) exceeds costs (demand). Or—heaven forbid—our business is unsuccessful because revenue (supply) is less than costs (demand). Or, thinking about resources, we (as a department, division, organization, or company) are trying to do too much with too few people or too little equipment. Or thinking in terms of time, there never seem to be enough hours in the day (supply) to do all the things we want to do, have to do, or have committed to do (demand).

A dance card is a way of investigating time from a supply-and-demand point of view. Just to get it out of the way, the term *dance card* is a reference to those more genteel days where, when ladies went to dances, they had dance cards showing the fixed number of dances that were available that night. Then, if a gentleman wanted to dance with a lady, he wrote his name against a particular dance—a waltz, tango, or whatever. Thus, that time slot was booked, if you want to think of it that way, and could not be booked by anyone else.

I hope you can see the analogy. You have a certain amount of time (or time slots) available every day, every week, every month, and every year. In work, at home, or wherever, certain of those slots get booked by other people—your boss, your customers, people who work for you, your children, your wife, husband, boyfriend, girlfriend, and so on. Given that, in general, there will be more demand on your time than you will be able to satisfy, how can you ensure that you put your time into the right things? The dance card, described shortly, is a tool for doing just that. It also has other uses, but let's see first what a dance card looks like. Figure 4.1 shows an example of a dance card.

I'm sure you can see it looks suspiciously like it was made using a spreadsheet. The second column lists all of the things that the owner of the dance card is involved in. The next two columns indicate how much work is estimated to go into these things over the period under investigation. Days per month (dpm), days per week (dpw), hours per day, or just plain days are all good ways of estimating how much work needs to be done. The remaining columns show how this work will be spread out over the period under investigation—in this case, eight months. There are two other items of interest. The top row shows how many days are available per month and also the total number of days available (160) over the entire period. Note that rather than trying to allow for the different numbers of working days in different countries, we have assumed that every month consists of 20 days. You could adjust this up or down for your own situation (e.g., December is definitely not 20 working days in most companies). The other item of interest is the total of all the work this dance card owner has to do—in this example, 289 days.

TOTAL DAYS AVAILABLE:	160			20	20	20	20	20	20	20	20
#	Project	Basis	Total	Nov	Dec	Jan	Feb	Mar	Apr	May	Jun
1	Project Abel	25 days	25	2.5	2.5	2.5	3.5	3.5	3.5	3.5	3.5
2	Project Baker	25 days	25	2.5	2.5	2.5	3.5	3.5	3.5	3.5	3.5
3	Project Charlie	2 dpm	16	2	2	2	2	2	2	2	2
4	Project Dog	1 dpw	40	5	5	5	5	5	5	5	5
5	E-mail	8 dpm	64	8	8	8	8	8	8	8	8
6	Training other people	1 dpm	8	1	1	1	1	1	1	1	1
7	Recruitment	1 dpm	8	1	1	1	1	1	1	1	1
8	Project Easy	10 days	10	2	2	1	1	1	1	1	1
9	Holidays	5 days	5		5						
10	Meetings	2.5 dpw	80	10	10	10	10	10	10	10	10
11	Training courses	2 days	2	0.5	0.5	1					
12	Trips	2 days	2			2					
13	Conference calls	0.5 dpm	4	0.5	0.5	0.5	0.5	0.5	0.5	0.5	0.5
	TOTAL DAYS WORK TO DO:	289		35.0	40.0	36.5	35.5	35.5	35.5	35.5	35.5

Figure 4.1 John's dance card.

Now in this example, the owner has some problems to address—if you'd call having twice as much work to do as time available to do it a problem, which I believe I would. We look at how one might address such a problem in one of the examples that follows. I hope you can see that the dance card is a good tool for—to begin with—understanding the sources of overcommitment. As it turns out, it is also a tool to begin fixing those problems, and we will see this shortly. Happily, there is also at least one other use we can put it to, which we will also see in the examples.

Maximizing the Strengths of the Team

One of the most foolish assumptions you could make would be that just because you have your sequence of events and you've given each job to a member of your crew, that it's all going to happen. Apart from the reasons already identified—confusion or overcommitment—there is the question of expertise and ability. Looking at it somewhat more broadly or holistically, we can think of it like this: Given that everybody has strengths and weaknesses, how can we ensure that we use as many of the strengths as possible and reduce the effects of the weaknesses?

I think you'll agree that libraries exist on this subject. Whole rainforests have been destroyed to provide the paper for the books, MBA theses, and the rest of the materials that have been written in this area. In keeping with our philosophy of finding a simple solution (Principle 1, "Many things are simple") however, I have used and found the following method to be very useful and effective. It's simple and it goes like this:

For each job allocated to a person, rate that allocation according to the following scheme:

1. **Superstar.** The person likes to do that particular job, has all the necessary skills, and will almost certainly deliver.

2. **Solid citizen**. The person is happy enough to do the job and knows how to do it. Maybe he or she doesn't get particularly fired up about doing it, but there's a pretty good chance he or she will deliver.

3. **Shaky**. For whatever reason—lack of motivation, lack of expertise, lack of time—there's a good chance this one isn't going to happen.

4. **Trainee**. This person is new to this task. The trainee needs hand holding, nurturing, mentoring, coaching, formal training, and micromanagement before you can be confident he or she will deliver.

5. **Goner**. It isn't going to happen. You need to find some other way of getting this job done.

Now, we can make a few observations about this scheme. The first is how do we know that a person falls into a particular category if we've never worked with him or her before? Simply give the person a few jobs from the sequence of events and see how he or she does. After two or three deliveries or nondeliveries, you'll have a much clearer idea.

Next, who should decide who falls into a particular category? There are two possibilities. You can decide and act accordingly. Alternatively—and this is better, but maybe harder to do—you and the person can rate his or her capabilities on particular jobs. Then you can compare notes and see where you might have not estimated the person's ability to deliver correctly.

Finally, what do the classifications mean for you? Well, the main thing they mean is that you will manage different situations differently. For example, you wouldn't manage a superstar the same way you would a trainee. In fact, the following are the leadership or management styles that would seem most appropriate in the different situations:

1. **Superstar**. The person likes to do that particular job, has all the necessary skills, and will almost certainly deliver. Leave them to get on with it with minimal intervention by you.

2. **Solid citizen**. The person is happy enough to do the job and knows how to do it. Maybe he or she doesn't get particularly fired up about doing it, but there's a pretty good chance he or she will deliver. Don't get too much in this person's way, but also don't assume it's all just going to happen.

3. **Shaky**. For whatever reason—lack of motivation, lack of expertise, lack of time—there's a good chance this one isn't going to happen. Establish—by giving the person a few jobs from the sequence of events and seeing the result—as quickly as you can whether it's going to happen or not. If it is, it becomes a 2; if not it becomes a 5.

4. **Trainee**. This person is new to this task. The trainee needs hand holding, nurturing, mentoring, coaching, formal training, and micromanagement before we can be confident he or she will deliver. Do all of these things to ensure you make them into at least a 2.

5. **Goner**. It isn't going to happen. You need to find some other way of getting this job done, *and* you need to deal with the person. Your choices are anything on the spectrum from firing to rehabilitation.

The Strip Board

The strip board is a very simple, very elegant, immensely powerful tool taken from the film industry. Its purpose is to show exactly who is doing exactly what and exactly when. You might argue that tools like Gantt charts (particularly if they're generated with fancy software packages like Microsoft Project) do precisely this. I argue in return that they do it, but not with anywhere near the accuracy, ease of use, or visibility of a strip board.

An example of a strip board section is shown in Figure 4.2. Another example of the use of a strip board in given in the "Examples" section.

Day #	Date	Cast [jobs] Bilbo	Frodo	Sam	Senior Designer	Gandalf
1	4-Sep-03					
2	5-Sep-03	Plan	Arrange meet	Design styling		
3	6-Sep-03			Design styling		
4	7-Sep-03			Design styling		
5	8-Sep-03	Agree site map with client	Agree site map with client	Agree site map with client		Agree site map with client
6	9-Sep-03					
7	10-Sep-03					
8	11-Sep-03			Concept development		
9	12-Sep-03			Interface development		
10	13-Sep-03	Internal design review	Internal design review	Amendments to design	Internal design review	
11	14-Sep-03	Client design presentation	Client design presentation	Client design presentation		Client design presentation
12	15-Sep-03			Client-driven changes		
13	16-Sep-03					
14	17-Sep-03					
15	18-Sep-03	Present design; get signoff	Present design; get signoff	Present design; get signoff		Present design; get signoff
16	19-Sep-03			Section thread design		
17	20-Sep-03			Section thread design		
18	21-Sep-03			Section thread design		
19	22-Sep-03	Present to client	Present to client			Present to client
20	23-Sep-03					
21	24-Sep-03					
22	25-Sep-03			Main site production		Main site production
23	26-Sep-03			Main site production		Main site production
24	27-Sep-03			Main site production		Main site production

Figure 4.2 A strip board.

Examples

Example 15: Getting a Life (Part 1)

One of the biggest problems in the developed world today is the problem of creating a balance between life and work. We work to live, yet if work takes up all our time, we have no life. Studies, articles, and books on this subject are starting to appear with increasing frequency, but we probably don't need studies to tell us that this has become a problem. Increased time spent getting to and from work, increasing pressures piled onto us at work ("If you don't do it, I'll find somebody who can"), and bringing work home with us all mean that our life is gradually being eroded by our work.

It is possible to stop this rot. I say this from experience, as someone who rarely works a week outside the range of 40–50 hours. To do so, you need three things. First of all, you need some kind of tool or measuring device to see how well or how badly you're doing. We've already seen this tool, the dance card. Next, you need to take on Principle 4, "Things don't get done if people don't do them." From this flows the notion that things don't get done if people don't have the time to do them. Thus, we must find ways to make the time available so that the right things get done. Finally—and this is the magic ingredient—you need the willpower to make this happen. If you really want to do it, it will happen, but you must *really* want to do it.

So let's take the dance card from Figure 4.1, let's give to it to it to a character we shall affectionately call Bozo, and let's reproduce it as Figure 4.3.

It doesn't take a rocket scientist to see that Bozo is a potential candidate for burnout. Even if he only began working this hard today—an unlikely assumption—his dance card shows that he has twice as much work to do as time available to do it. Nor is he in a situation where he has a hump to clear and once he clears that he'll be okay. Bozo isn't on a hump, he's on a plateau. On this plateau, as far as he can see into the

TOTAL DAYS AVAILABLE:	160			20	20	20	20	20	20	20	20
#	Project	Basis	Total	Nov	Dec	Jan	Feb	Mar	Apr	May	Jun
1	Project Abel	25 days	25	2.5	2.5	2.5	3.5	3.5	3.5	3.5	3.5
2	Project Baker	25 days	25	2.5	2.5	2.5	3.5	3.5	3.5	3.5	3.5
3	Project Charlie	2 dpm	16	2	2	2	2	2	2	2	2
4	Project Dog	1 dpw	40	5	5	5	5	5	5	5	5
5	E-mail (2 days per week)	8 dpm	64	8	8	8	8	8	8	8	8
6	Training other people	1 dpm	8	1	1	1	1	1	1	1	1
7	Recruitment	1 dpm	8	1	1	1	1	1	1	1	1
8	Project Easy	10 days	10	2	2	1	1	1	1	1	1
9	Holidays	5 days	5		5						
10	Meetings	2.5 dpw	80	10	10	10	10	10	10	10	10
11	Training courses	2 days	2	0.5	0.5	1					
12	Trips	2 days	2			2					
13	Conference calls	0.5 dpm	4	0.5	0.5	0.5	0.5	0.5	0.5	0.5	0.5
	TOTAL DAYS WORK TO DO:	289		35.0	40.0	36.5	35.5	35.5	35.5	35.5	35.5
	Overload:	81%									

Figure 4.3 Bozo's dance card.

future, quite literally as long as he stays in that job, he has twice as much work to do as he has time available to do it. This isn't all: Unless he does something about this, then (a) it will never get better, and (b) it can only get worse. This is Bozo's starting point and because of this gloomy prognosis, he decides to do something about. The fact that his children didn't recognize him recently and his wife thinks she has a lodger rather than a husband further spur him on to try to resolve the problem.

Now, there are only two things Bozo can do to fix this supply–demand problem: He can increase the supply or decrease the demand. Increasing the supply means making more hours available, but these are hours that Bozo will have to take out of his personal life. He decides that this is no longer an option for him.

If he is not going to increase supply, then he must decrease demand. That is, he must find ways of doing less work. There are three ways he can do this:

- Find smarter ways to do particular things. For example, he might be able to delegate things.

- Don't do particular things in the period under investigation.

- Don't do particular things at all.

The way we approach this problem is with a series of interventions (as a doctor might say), starting with those that are easy to implement and building up to much more radical ones. You can go straight to the radical ones if you prefer, but a gentler slope might suit you better.

We're first going to explore some "work smarter" options. When somebody's personal supply–demand equation is as out of whack as Bozo's is, it is pointless to look at the things that consume small amounts of his time (for example, the categories "Training courses" or "Trips" take up only 2 days). We need to look at the big hitters like "Meetings" (80 days) or "E-mail" (64 days). (E-mail can be taken to include all forms of material arriving in Bozo's inbox, including those normal interruptions that are part of any working day.) We discover, from talking to Bozo, that he deals with every interruption when it comes in. In essence, he tries to operate an empty-at-all-times inbox. Our first job is to wean him off this habit.

We suggest to him that instead of doing this he limit himself to checking his inbox twice a day, once in the morning and once in the afternoon, for an hour each time. He should also turn off the e-mail notification on his computer. Two hours a day is 10 hours a week (i.e., 1.25 days per week instead of 2 days per week as he currently has). Using this simple strategy he saves 0.75 days per week, which is 3 days per month (assuming 4 weeks in a month), which is 24 days over the period. Such a change in Bozo's behavior is unlikely to go unnoticed for too long. Sooner or later, somebody will ask him, "Didn't you read my e-mail?" He should then explain that he now only reads his e-mail twice a day, from (say) 9:00–10:00 a.m. and 2:00–3:00 p.m. This is useful information (not to mention a useful tip) for the colleague, and the issue should end there. Bozo is now ready for the next dose of medicine, which is a bit heavier.

There are two alternative treatments at this point. One would be to reduce the twice-a-day routine to once a day. This would half the 24 days for e-mail to 12 days. However, hard-core e-mail junkies might find this difficult to do. So an alternative—and happily, it's even more effective—is to do the following. Twice a day, as we have described, sweep your e-mail. This time, however, rather than spending an hour on it, just deal with those ones that are important and urgent (i.e., they *must* be done today). Leave everything else. Bozo does this, tentatively at first and then more confidently, and finally, he is brutal as to what *must* be done today. He thus reduces his time spent on e-mail and inbox interruptions to no more than 1 day per week, 4 days per month, or 32 days in the period under investigation. Bozo's colleagues will merely notice that Bozo has become somewhat less tolerant of (relatively) unimportant interruptions and issues. To put it another way, Bozo only deals with things that are important.

Now, it turns out that there are even more radical things he can do. If you remember, Bozo's original philosophy amounted to checking everything that came in, in case there was something important, and trying to keep a clear inbox. A different approach would be to say, "If something is important enough, I need to find out about it and not worry about the rest of the stuff in the inbox." To implement this, you could take the following approach: Check your inbox once a day—or you could even (gasp!) go to Monday, Wednesday, and Friday or even (bigger gasp!) just Monday and Friday. If something is important and urgent or must be done today, do it. Otherwise just leave it to rot in your inbox. When your inbox is full, empty it, either by going through it item by item or—better still—by trashing the lot and starting again. Will you have missed something important? Why don't you do it and see what happens? If you did miss something important, you can do your inbox sweeping more often. If you didn't, you could consider doing it even (gasp again!) less often.

Getting back to Bozo, his dance card now looks like the one shown in Figure 4.4.

Let's leave Bozo for a moment and talk about you. If you try these things, they will have the same effect. If you try them, you might fall by the wayside at first, but if you persevere and make these simple procedures part of your working day, you will find that a lot of time gets saved. It will also make you confident enough about your ability to change your own behaviors that you might be prepared to try the next batch of medicine, which is a bit more severe. By the same token, if you haven't mastered these techniques I've just described, it is unlikely that you'll have the stomach for what follows.

TOTAL DAYS AVAILABLE:	160			20	20	20	20	20	20	20	20
#	Project	Basis	Total	Nov	Dec	Jan	Feb	Mar	Apr	May	Jun
1	Project Abel	25 days	25	2.5	2.5	2.5	3.5	3.5	3.5	3.5	3.5
2	Project Baker	25 days	25	2.5	2.5	2.5	3.5	3.5	3.5	3.5	3.5
3	Project Charlie	2 dpm	16	2	2	2	2	2	2	2	2
4	Project Dog	1 dpw	40	5	5	5	5	5	5	5	5
5	E-mail (1 day per week)	4 dpm	32	4	4	4	4	4	4	4	4
6	Training other people	1 dpm	8	1	1	1	1	1	1	1	1
7	Recruitment	1 dpm	8	1	1	1	1	1	1	1	1
8	Project Easy	10 days	10	2	2	1	1	1	1	1	1
9	Holidays	5 days	5		5						
10	Meetings	2.5 dpw	80	10	10	10	10	10	10	10	10
11	Training courses	2 days	2	0.5	0.5	1					
12	Trips	2 days	2			2					
13	Conference calls	0.5 dpm	4	0.5	0.5	0.5	0.5	0.5	0.5	0.5	0.5
	TOTAL DAYS WORK TO DO:	257		31.0	36.0	32.5	31.5	31.5	31.5	31.5	31.5
	Overload:	61%									

Figure 4.4 Bozo's dance card with e-mail sorted.

Example 16: Getting a Life (Part 2)

Let's return to Bozo. As we said in the previous example, we still haven't begun to administer the really heavy medicine. At 61 percent overload, Bozo is still in an unhealthy position. Let's assume that he pretty much has no more "work smarter" options. There is nobody to whom he can delegate anything. The meetings and conference calls, both of which consume an extraordinary amount of his time, are all short, necessary events (because of the nature of his job). So neither the meetings nor the conference calls are long, rambling, out-of-control things that could be tightened up with good agendas, decent chairing, and action items. It's now time to look at our two other approaches to reducing demand:

- Don't do particular things in the period under investigation.

- Don't do particular things at all.

It is true to say that there is one way we could automatically, as it were, balance the supply and demand on Bozo's dance card. If Bozo were to prioritize the items on his dance card and make a cut at the point where he ran out of supply, then the problem would be solved (at least from the numbers point of view). Without prejudging whether this would be a good thing to do, let's prioritize the items on Bozo's dance card. We'll use the what-if-we-could-only-do-one-thing test that was described earlier. After a lot of agonizing on Bozo's part, let's assume the result is as shown in Figure 4.5.

The extra column we have added in to Bozo's dance card shows that—in theory, at least—he should really only do his first five priorities and stop after that. I should say at this point that this is a valid suggestion and should not be dismissed out of hand. I'll agree that it's very strong medicine, but if you have the stomach for it, it completely solves the problem. Let's assume, however, that this is much too radical a thing to do. So where do we go from here?

#	Project	Basis	Total	Cumulative	20 Nov	20 Dec	20 Jan	20 Feb	20 Mar	20 Apr	20 May	20 Jun
	TOTAL DAYS AVAILABLE:	160										
1	Project Dog	1 dpw	40	40	5	5	5	5	5	5	5	5
2	Project Abel	25 days	25	65	2.5	2.5	2.5	3.5	3.5	3.5	3.5	3.5
3	Project Baker	25 days	25	90	2.5	2.5	2.5	3.5	3.5	3.5	3.5	3.5
4	Project Charlie	2 dpm	16	106	2	2	2	2	2	2	2	2
5	Meetings	2.5 dpw	80	186	10	10	10	10	10	10	10	10
6	E-mail (1 day per week)	4 dpm	32	218	4	4	4	4	4	4	4	4
7	Conference calls	0.5 dpm	4	222	0.5	0.5	0.5	0.5	0.5	0.5	0.5	0.5
8	Project Easy	10 days	10	232	2	2	1	1	1	1	1	1
9	Vacation	5 days	5	237		5						
10	Training courses	2 days	2	239	0.5	0.5	1					
11	Recruitment	1 dpm	8	247	1	1	1	1	1	1	1	1
12	Training other people	1 dpm	8	255	1	1	1	1	1	1	1	1
13	Trips	2 days	2	257			2					
	TOTAL DAYS WORK TO DO:	257			31.0	36.0	32.5	31.5	31.5	31.5	31.5	31.5
	Overload:	61%										

Figure 4.5 Bozo's prioritized dance card.

Well, an important factor that we haven't considered so far is on what Bozo's performance is being measured. Do we know which of the items in his list will become the basis for his performance appraisal or evaluation? Let's assume they're as shown in Figure 4.6. (Note that we've grouped the key performance areas together. Also, although Bozo's boss might not regard Bozo's vacation as a key performance area, Bozo does!)

Now, what are we to make of this picture? What realistic actions can we take as a result? This is where it's going to get tough for Bozo.

Whichever way you look at this, Bozo is overworked. There are then two possibilities: Either this is a hump or it isn't. It is a hump if some of Bozo's projects will end. Let's say, for example, that projects Dog, Able, and Baker will all end at the end of June. This would mean that, with these gone, Bozo's workload would drop to 167 days and provided he didn't take on anything new, he'd be in business. The other possibility—that this is not a hump—simply means that Bozo is doing the work of more than one person, which is not a tenable situation in the long term.

Now, I hope that you can see that in both of these cases, the problem facing Bozo is essentially the same. He must convince his boss that, in the first case, he cannot take on any or much new work when the current hump is cleared; in the second case, he needs to shed some work. He must do a sales job. How will he do this?

To sell his boss on either of these notions, there must be something in it for his boss. That magic ingredient can be deduced from the principle we have been describing throughout this chapter: Principle 4, "Things don't get done if people don't do them." Bozo's approach to his boss uses this as a jumping-off point. It goes something like this.

If Bozo's dance card is as shown in Figure 4.6, then he does not have enough time to do all of the things he is meant to do and on which he will be measured. "Continuous or extended overtime is not the answer," Bozo states. "Says who?" his boss replies, using that if-it's-good-enough-for-me-it's-good-enough-for-everyone-else tone of voice.

TOTAL DAYS AVAILABLE:	160					20	20	20	20	20	20	20	20
#	Key Performance Area	Project	Basis	Total	Cumulative	Nov	Dec	Jan	Feb	Mar	Apr	May	Jun
1	Yes	Project Dog	1 dpw	40	40	5	5	5	5	5	5	5	5
2	Yes	Project Abel	25 days	25	65	2.5	2.5	2.5	3.5	3.5	3.5	3.5	3.5
3	Yes	Project Baker	25 days	25	90	2.5	2.5	2.5	3.5	3.5	3.5	3.5	3.5
4	Yes	Project Charlie	2 dpm	16	106	2	2	2	2	2	2	2	2
5	Yes	Meetings	2.5 dpw	80	186	10	10	10	10	10	10	10	10
6	Yes	Project Easy	10 days	10	196	2	2	1	1	1	1	1	1
7	Yes	Training courses	2 days	2	198	0.5	0.5	1					
8	Yes	Recruitment	1 dpm	8	206	1	1	1	1	1	1	1	1
9	Yes	Training other people	1 dpm	8	214	1	1	1	1	1	1	1	1
10	Yes	Vacation	5 days	5	219		5						
11		E-mail (1 day per week)	4 dpm	32	251	4	4	4	4	4	4	4	4
12		Conference calls	0.5 dpm	4	255	0.5	0.5	0.5	0.5	0.5	0.5	0.5	0.5
13		Trips	2 days	2	257			2					
		TOTAL DAYS WORK TO DO:	257			31.0	36.0	32.5	31.5	31.5	31.5	31.5	31.5
		Overload:	61%										

Figure 4.6 Bozo's prioritized dance card showing key performance areas.

"Says him," says Bozo, throwing on the table a copy of *The Deadline* by Tom DeMarco [1]. In it, in Chapter 15, under the heading "The Effects of Pressure" it says some scary things:

- People under pressure don't think any faster.

- Extended overtime is a productivity-reduction tactic.

- Short bursts of pressure and even overtime may be a useful tactic as they focus people and increase the sense that the work is important, but extended pressure is always a mistake.

- Perhaps managers make so much use of pressure because they don't know what else to do, or are daunted by how difficult the alternatives are.

- Terrible suspicion: The real reason for use of pressure and overtime may be to make everyone look better when the project fails.

Bozo particularly enjoys saying the last two to his boss.

"So who's he anyway?" the boss asks. Then Bozo goes at it from another angle. "When I'm overloaded like this, I'm like a gladiator," he says. "Each time I go out in the arena I may succeed in surviving. But sooner or later, I'm going to fail. And when I fail, you fail. This is inevitable as long as I stay at this level of overload. If, however, I can get back to an acceptable level (Bozo needs to have defined what this is. It might be, for example, he has decided that *maximum* 50-hour weeks would be an acceptable level to work at. This would be an overload level of at most 25 percent representing a demand target in the range of 160–200 days [i.e., 160 days + 25%]), then in return I can *guarantee* you that I will always be able to deliver on my commitments. Which would you like? The uncertainty of a gladiator or the certainty of somebody who always delivers?"

It might be that Bozo wins the argument at this point, and that the sales job is done. What's maybe more likely though, is that the boss isn't buying. This is when Bozo's will to succeed in his quest to get a life will be tested to the limit. You see, the nice thing about all of this is that logic is on Bozo's side. Jobs *don't* get done if people don't do them. Bozo has the proof positive—on his dance card—that there are certain things on which his performance is being measured that he has little or no chance of achieving. In the example in Figure 4.6, given that e-mails and conference calls must both be done in addition to the key performance areas, and that all projects are ongoing for the next 8 months, Bozo has to lose two projects, say Abel and Baker. If he could do this, he would be down to 207 days, which would be close to the 25 percent overload level we spoke of earlier.

So now, he must take the bold step of telling his boss that he'll have to find some other way of doing this because Bozo can't do it. His boss will bluster, of course, and behave like the Beadle when Oliver Twist asked for some more soup [2], but there's nothing he can do if Bozo holds firm. Again you might feel this medicine is too strong for you. In that case you can go for the milder, but no less effective version—it just takes longer to take effect—that you will endure whatever you have at the moment until those things end, but you won't take on any new things. Your justification for refusing things each time they are offered will be that you are already overloaded.

You have to understand that people will continue to throw stuff over to you if you let them. In general they do this because they have no reason to believe there's a problem. You haven't told them there's a problem. If you don't tell them, there's no reason they should know. If you tell them, they must find other ways to solve it. Productivity reduction tactics make no sense when you understand what a productivity reduction tactic actually is. It says that you will work long, stressful hours and you will achieve less than if you had worked a straight 40-hour week. Such a thing makes no sense whatsoever for you, your customers, your employer, your boss, your company, your division, your department, your organization, or anybody else.

This is the true test of Bozo's moral fiber. Hold firm and eventually they must back down. Appear to sway, show any weakness and they will assume—rightly so—that you have agreed to return to the old patterns of behavior. However, if you hold firm you will be the winner. I say this both from personal experience and from having seen other people succeed at it. Jobs don't get done if people don't do them. It all flows from this.

Finally, three other things might help you. First, read Example 19 later in this chapter. It covers a situation in which the organization is trying to do too much with too little resources. It might be that the problem of which you are the victim has to be solved at an organizational level rather than an individual one.

Second, in an example in Chapter 7, I describe a negotiation method where, rather than the negotiation being some kind of argument, it becomes a problem-solving session. The two sides have a mutual problem—in this case, you're working too hard and your boss needs to get many things done—and you try to find creative ways to ease *both* of your pains. The important thing in this negotiation method is that any solution you come up with has to be assessable on some objective basis. Dance cards provide you with a way of assessing the various solutions objectively. For example, you might want to ensure that you share some of the pain with your boss, that you're not the only one who gets to ease their overload situation.

Third, if you want to read a fictionalized account of somebody winning one of these negotiations in trying circumstances, you could read the worked example sections in one of my other books, *How to Run Successful Projects in Web Time* [3].

Example 17: Aligning Goals or Objectives

One of the problems that occurs often in business is when you have, say, a bunch of people working for you (e.g., on a project or in a department) and what they do is not what you expect. This can be negative for a couple of reasons. First of all—clearly—you didn't get to where you expected to be. Second, and often more important, you don't find this out until much too late.

Many ways have been devised to try and address this situation, including management by objectives—sometimes involving almost lawyer-like definition of objectives, balanced score cards, and key performance indicators, to name but a few. In my experience, dance cards represent a far better way to go about this. Here's how you go about it:

1. Get each of the people who work for you to do a dance card to cover the period you're interested in.

2. Now go through the dance cards with each person in turn. Go through them line by line.

3. Understand what they're intending to do over the period.

4. Look at the supply and demand and see how realistic what they're proposing to do is. If they're as overloaded as Bozo was in the last example—even the Bozo of Figure 4.6—then there's a fair chance that the things they're proposing to do won't happen. There's no fun in finding this out; better to find it out now than down the line. Note, too, that from the point of view of you as a manager, this approach is a far more sensible, civilized, and effective way of dealing with supply–demand problems than the adversarial approach described in the preceding example.

5. Correct any things that don't line up with your expectations, so that you get a final agreed-on (by both parties) dance card that has a reasonable supply–demand balance.

6. Now let them loose, and you can be much more confident that their contribution to your success will be the one you wanted.

Example 18: Ensuring a Project or Endeavor Gets Done

It seems to me that there is a view in much of the business world that when you undertake something new, that you do whatever planning you can, and after that it's in the lap of the gods. In fact, increasingly these days, with everyone fussing about how things have speeded up and how everything is changing so quickly, there seems to be a tendency to say, "We don't have time to plan, just go do it." This is a view that would not, in general, be shared by some other disciplines. The military, for example, or the movie industry are disciplines in which every attempt is made to remove as much uncertainty as possible from the proceedings to maximize everyone's chances of success. Maybe it's because in the military, lives are often at stake, whereas in film-making, such huge amounts of money are involved that great care is taken to reduce the dead hand of chance. For us exponents of common sense, I would argue that removing the dead hand of chance as much as possible is a good thing to do. It means that we bring the maximum sense of reality into whatever venture we are beginning. It means that everyone's expectations are set correctly. It means we have the best chance of doing what we promised to do.

One of the best ways to remove the hand of chance is to lay out your venture on a strip board. In doing this notice that we combine use of three of the four principles we have described so far (Principle 2, "Know what you're trying to do"; Principle 3, "There is always a sequence of events"; and Principle 4, "Things don't get done if people don't do them").

To illustrate laying out a venture on a strip board, let me use the following example. We are a company who has a new product that has emerged from our research department. The research people think it's hot and it's agreed that one of the ways we can test this hypothesis is to find some people who want to buy it. (Notice here the use again of our first principle of common sense, "Many things are simple." It might be that the marketing department is going to do all kinds of fancy market research on this product, and although in no way do I mean to knock that, there's nothing like finding some people prepared to part with some hard cash as a way of testing the market.)

Anyway, back to our product. We agree first on the scope of this little trial (Principle 2, "Know what you're trying to do"). We use the "understand what you're trying to do" and "know if what you're trying to do is what everyone wants" tools described in Chapter 2. Using these, we establish that the goals of the venture that will keep all of the stakeholders happy are those in the following list. We agree that we will run the show for three months. At the end of that time, if the following goals have been achieved, the project will be classified as a success:

- Get some revenue. (We agree that we will try to at least cover our costs during this exercise.)

- Get some customers (i.e., reference sites).

- Develop some basic marketing materials, sales materials, and a sales approach.

- Make some recommendations about what, if any, changes are needed to make the product more saleable.

We also make clear that the following are *not* part of the scope of our project:

- Complete, final marketing and sales collateral.

- Making changes to the product to make it more saleable. (We will make *recommendations*, but not the changes themselves. In other words, we go with whatever research they have given us.)

Now, using Principles 3 ("There is always a sequence of events") and 4 ("Things don't get done if people don't do them"), we lay out all of the jobs we can think of onto a strip board as shown in Figure 4.7.

Day #	Date	Cast [jobs]			
		Strider	Gilgalad	Frodo	Gandalf
1	14-Nov-03	Scoping plan	Scoping plan; writing first draft of project plan	3 hrs follow-up on mailer	Establish Web requirements
2	15-Nov-03		Establish Web requirements; enter them into plan	3 hrs follow-up on mailer	
3	16-Nov-03		Talk to AB on accounts	3 hrs follow-up on mailer	
4	17-Nov-03		N/A	3 hrs follow-up on mailer	
5	18-Nov-03				
6	19-Nov-03				
7	20-Nov-03		Talk to ABE on DE, FG on accounts, Sales meeting		
8	21-Nov-03		N/A	3 hrs follow-up on mailer	
9	22-Nov-03		N/A	3 hrs follow-up on mailer	
10	23-Nov-03	Meet those guys	Meet those guys; ABC on defining Web requirements;	3 hrs follow-up on mailer	
11	24-Nov-03		Requirements of proj; meet DE on marketing requirements	3 hrs follow-up on mailer	
12	25-Nov-03				
13	26-Nov-03				
14	27-Nov-03		Sales meeting (present the plan); practice ABC presentation		
15	28-Nov-03		On the phone	3 hrs follow-up on mailer	
16	29-Nov-03	Written "reference" to Webfactory	On the phone; test ABC presentation	3 hrs follow-up on mailer	
17	30-Nov-03	Meet other guys		3 hrs follow-up on mailer	

Figure 4.7 Jobs laid out on a strip board.

Now we see precisely who's doing what and when. We can test key assumptions—we've assumed, for example, that we are going to target 100 customers and that we will achieve a conversion rate of calls to meetings of, say, 20 percent. This means we have to attend 20 meetings over the duration of the project at, say, two a day, so we can see from the strip board if enough time has been set aside for meetings. If we achieve a conversion rate of meetings to sales of, say, one in two, then we can estimate the revenue that will flow from our efforts and see if it satisfies the goals we identified earlier. Also using the strip board, everyone can see very clearly the big picture and his or her part in it. It will be easy for us to check progress. On any given day, we can draw a horizontal line and anything above that line should be done. If some things are not, then we are behind schedule; if some things from below the line are done, then we are ahead of schedule.

The hand of chance will still intervene in our project, of that there is no doubt, but now when it does, we won't have that uncertain feeling of what it means, or what it will do to us. Using our strip board we'll be able to see precisely what the inevitable surprises on the project will do to us.

In reality, a strip board is like a simulator of your venture. By building or working through a strip board, you can get a real feeling of what it would be like to live through the project. In addition, you can try all manner of scenarios before you encounter them for real.

Example 19: Ensuring That Your Organization Delivers on Its Commitments

Do you have any of the following problems?

- You work in the product development or service delivery parts of your organization. From your point of view, it seems as if the people who are responsible for promising or committing things to customers always make unreasonable promises.

- You are a salesperson or a person responsible for ensuring that promised customer service levels are achieved. It seems like the product development or service delivery people in your organization never seem to come through on the commitments you have made. This seems to be true even when (a) you feel you have made eminently reasonable promises, and (b) you might have even gone to the trouble of checking with the appropriate people: "Are you absolutely sure I can feel confident in promising this?"

- You are the head of an organization of the types just described. You have a feeling that you are not getting enough bang for the buck, that somehow—though you can't quite see how—your organization is inefficient, or even—your darkest fear—inept; that it doesn't really know what it's about. You've tried lots of things—training, changes in management structure or personnel, quality improvement drives and programs—but the basic problem seems to remain.

- You are anyone in the organization and you find yourself working harder and harder and every day becoming more and more stressful.

If you answered "Yes" to any of these questions, then your problem might be that your organization-wide demand exceeds supply. Put more simply, it means that you might be trying to do too much with too little. "What's new?" I hear you ask, and I can understand why you might say that. Most organizations do. Indeed, there is an argument that says it's a good thing to do; that all organizations should strive such that their reach exceeds their grasp. For example, in a *Fortune* article titled "Reinvent Your Company," [4] the author Gary Hamel says that the first rule for designing a culture that inspires innovation is to set unreasonable expectations. He quotes a GE Capital executive as saying, "It is expected that we will grow earnings 20 percent per year or more. When you have objectives that are that outlandish, it forces you to think very differently about your opportunities."

Now, I have no problem with any of this. Ambitious targets? Sure. Thinking innovatively about achieving them? Absolutely. But not at the expense of losing the plot, and certainly not by trying to pretend that our fourth principle of common sense ("Things don't get done if people don't do them") somehow doesn't apply to you. I'll state it as bluntly as I can: If your organization is trying to do more work than there are people available to do it, then you will end up not doing all of the things that need to be done. Depending on the shortfall between demand (work to be done) and supply (people available to do it), you might end up missing your targets by a little bit or by a mile.

In my experience, the tendency is more toward the latter end of the spectrum. Organizations that have a supply–demand discrepancy usually have a huge one. This is particularly true, I have found, of fast-growth, high-tech organizations, especially if they have large amounts of somebody else's money paying for their endeavors.

So what should you do? It's very simple, really. We've seen the approach already in this chapter. Figure out as an organization how much demand there is (work to be done), figure out how much supply there is (people to do the work), prioritize the list, and then make the cuts. Forget about all those notions of extended overtime or "stretch" (where stretch generally equals impossible or insane) targets. They quite simply don't work on any kind of sustainable basis. I provide an example in the tables that follow. Table 4.1 lists a hypothetical (product development, in this case) organization's projects together with the estimated amount of work in each project. Let's assume that they are looking at say, a 12-month period.

Now let's assume that the same organization has a total amount of time available to it of 1,892 person-weeks over the same period. This takes into account people already on the payroll plus those who will be hired during the same period. I think you can see that this organization has a big problem. I hope you can see that if you worked in such an organization, all of the scenarios I described at the beginning of this example would be happening.

Table 4.1 Organization-wide supply–demand.

Project		Work or Effort (in person-weeks)
1	Project Able	8
2	Project Baker	541
3	Project Charlie	48
4	Project Dog	440
5	Project Easy	368
6	Project Foxtrot	135
7	Project Golf	976
8	Project Hotel	1,032
9	Project India	256
10	Support of existing products (Estimates based on so many weeks per product)	392
11	R&D (Estimate based on so many people for so many weeks)	176
12	Training (Estimate based on so much training per person)	96
Subtotal		4,468
Project Management Effort @ 10%		447
Contingency @15%		670
Total		5,585

Now to fix this problem—as the organization must—it must make the cut at the point at which supply matches demand. To make the cut, this organization will have to do the following:

- Continue (presumably) to include support, R&D, and training among those things that have to be done.

- Continue to add in the project management and contingency overheads.

- Decide which of the remaining projects it intends to do, so that the total of the projects plus support, R&D, training, project management, and contingency doesn't exceed 1,892 person-weeks.

Will this be a pleasant exercise? Not likely. When they realize all of the things that aren't going to get done, I suspect it will be distinctly unpleasant. Do they have to do it? Yes, I would argue that they do. What will happen to them if they don't do it? Well, you might remember we referred earlier to the hand of chance. If this (hypothetical, although maybe not as hypothetical or as rare as you would have hoped) organization doesn't consciously and explicitly decide what it wants to do, chance will decide for it. If you think that that's a good way for an organization to conduct its business and go about achieving its goals, there's not a lot I can add.

Just to add one small footnote to this example, you'll notice that we implicitly assumed that we were dealing with one sort of person or skill level. A person-week of any product developer's time was equivalent to that of any other product developer, and we were able to count them all up in one big bucket. In solving an organization's supply–demand problems, we first need to solve the problem at this level. When we have done that we can move a level down, where we look at how much of particular skill sets we need. For example, again in a product development organization, we might have to consider how many designers, developers, testers, and so on, that we'll need.

Example 20: Coping with Interruptions

Have you ever thought how uncomplicated your working life would be if there were no interruptions? You'd plan your week by establishing exactly what needed to get done, there would be ample time for everything, and you would travel home on Friday evening with a glow of self-satisfaction and a song in your heart.

Sadly, the world isn't like that, and your beautifully crafted plan for the week can end up so battered by surprises, interruptions, and firefights that you travel home on Friday wondering how it could possibly be Friday already and where the week has gone.

It might surprise you to know that you already know the cure for this. It's what I think of as the "hot date" scenario: Imagine that on a particular day you had a hot date. To be as bland and politically correct as possible, let's just describe it as a meeting that you *must* go to. You have no alternative but to go to this meeting. Now how would you organize your day in these circumstances? Isn't it true that you would plan your day as accurately as you could, allowing strict time slots to accomplish each thing that needed to be done? But you would also do something else. Knowing how easy it is for somebody to spring surprises on you or interrupt you, you would actually allow time for this. Let's say you had to leave the office no later than 5 p.m. to make your hot date; you wouldn't plan to be finished by then. That would be much too risky. Instead, you would plan to be finished by, say, 4 p.m., and then you could either leave at that point, or the extra hour would be there to save your bacon if something came up.

Now, even though we know this, it is not something we do every day. Indeed, we have a tendency to do completely the opposite. Even though we know from bitter experience that every day there are interruptions, we behave as if today—for some bizarre reason—there will be no interruptions at all. Moreover, we are surprised and unhappy when these interruptions then occur, even though all logic tells us that they were bound to happen.

To deal with interruptions, the common-sense thing to do is to apply the hot date scenario every day. Here's a simple and very powerful way to do so:

1. Record, for a given week, the amount of time each day that you put into dealing with interruptions.

2. From this, compute a daily average.

3. This is the amount of time you should put into every day when you are planning your day.

Table 4.2 provides an illustration. Let's say that for a particular week, you record the following by way of time spent servicing interruptions.

Table 4.2 Calculating daily interruption time.

Day	Mon.	Tue.	Wed.	Thur.	Fri.
Time spent (in hours)	2	8	.5	1.5	3

Thus, the daily average is 3 hours, or

$$\frac{2 + 8 + .5 + 1.5 + 3}{5}$$

This means that on the basis of this evidence you are likely to spend 3 hours per day servicing interruptions. By factoring this into your time planning (e.g., you could do it on a dance card), you can ensure that the day's interruptions don't compromise the things you really have to get done. A day like the Tuesday illustrated in Table 4.2 will still leave your day in tatters, but that's better than having every day end in tatters!

Example 21: Managing in Recessionary Times

Read this quote: "Colgate-Palmolive has a remarkable record of improving productivity, as reflected in gross margin, virtually every year for the past 15 years, even during the last recession. The process is ingrained, and it pays off impressively: In the brutally competitive, slow-growing business of household products, Colgate's stock has risen an average of 28 percent annually over the past five years." [5] The article from which this is taken makes the point that during a slow-down or recession, productivity typically goes through the floor. It goes on to say that you need to stop this from happening and, in fact, to cause the opposite to happen. Not only does this see you through the downturn, but it puts you in a stronger position when things turn up.

No matter what business you are in, avoiding waste is one way to improve productivity. In Examples 17 and 19, you saw two very powerful ways of avoiding waste. Aligning goals using dance cards ensures that nobody spends time on wild goose chases or does things that take them directions they don't want to go. Planning using strip boards ensures that we use every day wisely and don't create situations in which ventures get held up because somebody wasn't there to do something when they were needed.

So What Should You Do?

1. Keep a list of all of the projects, ventures, endeavors, and undertakings for which you are responsible.

2. Make sure that after every meeting or phone call, and for every project, venture, endeavor, or undertaking, that there is a sequence of events (Principle 3, "There is always a sequence of events"). For each job in the sequence, ensure that there is somebody available to do it when the time comes for it to be done.

3. Maximize the strengths of the people you are working with. (Not necessarily just subordinates, either. The same idea will work with bosses, customers, peers, or anybody else.)

4. Keep a dance card and use it to get a life if you don't already have one, using the ideas described in Example 15.

5. Teach dance cards to those who work for you. Then use the dance cards to align their objectives with yours.

6. You can do the same with your peers. This will show you if what all of you are planning to do meshes with what your management are expecting and what they have committed your organization to doing.

7. Use strip boards as your method of choice for planning projects, ventures, endeavors, and undertakings. Use them in preference to Gantt charts and, in particular, use them in preference to so-called project management tools. (Microsoft Project is an example of these.) Strip boards can be built using any spreadsheet package, such as Microsoft Excel.

8. Do the organization-wide supply–demand calculations for your organization. Then make the cut.

9. Build time for interruptions into your day.

PRINCIPLE 1: MANY THINGS ARE SIMPLE

PRINCIPLE 2: KNOW WHAT YOU'RE TRYING TO DO

PRINCIPLE 3: THERE IS ALWAYS A SEQUENCE OF EVENTS

PRINCIPLE 4: THINGS DON'T GET DONE IF PEOPLE DON'T DO THEM

References

1. DeMarco, Tom, *The Deadline: A Novel About Project Management*, New York: Dorset House, 1997, p. 199.

2. Dickens, Charles, *Oliver Twist*, New York: Tor Books, 1998.

3. O'Connell, Fergus, *How to Run Successful Projects in Web Time*, Boston: Artech House, 2000.

4. Hamel, Gary, "Reinvent Your Company," *Fortune*, June 12, 2000, p. 106.

5. Charan, Ram and Colvin, Geoffrey, "Managing for the Slowdown," *Fortune*, February 5, 2001. Also at *http://www.business2.com/articles/mag/0,1640,9247,00.html*.

5

THINGS RARELY TURN
OUT AS EXPECTED

Despite our best efforts, there will always be surprises. This chapter talks about minimizing the number and effect of surprises.

Questions

1. Why should you have contingency or margin for error in your plans?

   (a) Because you'd be mad not to.

   (b) To be able to deal with unexpected things.

   (c) To be able to contain the effect of unexpected things within your project and stop them from affecting related projects.

   (d) Because you'll almost invariably use it.

2. True or false?

   (a) Contingency is mandatory on any project, venture, or endeavor.

   (b) It's okay to hide contingency in a plan if that's the only way you can ensure it stays in.

   (c) Adding time onto the schedule is a way of putting contingency into it.

   (d) Grouping things into "have to have" and "nice to have" categories is a way of finding contingency.

3. True or false?

   (a) If you have contingency in your plans, then there's no need for you to do risk analysis.

   (b) Risk analysis techniques are all about higher mathematics, algorithms, and rocket science.

   (c) In assessing a particular risk, one of the main factors to consider is the likelihood of the risk happening.

   (d) In assessing a particular risk, one of the main factors to consider is the impact that risk will have if it should happen.

Answers

1. (a) 5 points

I mean it to be literally true. If you believe that things will turn out precisely as you predicted—despite the fact that this has probably never happened to anyone in their whole life—then you must be mad!

(b) 5 points

Yes.

(c) 5 points

Yes. Let's say, for example, you're developing a product and the marketing department has built a product launch plan based on delivery dates you have given them. If your plan contains no contingency and it slips, you potentially mess up their entire plan. With contingency, you might be able to contain the effect of your slippages without passing it on.

(d) 5 points

Yes. I don't think I've ever seen a plan where the contingency wasn't used.

2. (a) 5 points

True, for all of the reasons described in Question 1.

(b) 5 points

For me, true. If the morality of this disturbs you, then put the contingency explicitly into the plan and don't let anybody (bosses, customers, peers, your team, or anyone else) make you take it out.

(c) 5 points

Yes, it's true.

(d) 5 points

True. It will help, provided you only commit to delivering the "have to haves" and use the "nice to haves" as things you might or might not be able to do.

3. (a) 5 points

False. It's far better to do both.

(b) 5 points

False, as you'll see shortly.

(c) 5 points

True.

(d) 5 points

True.

Scores

60 points   Wow!

35–59 points   Good performance. Not too many flies on you.

Less than 35 points   Where's that flyswatter?

The Idea

Life is full of surprises. Not a week goes by that we don't find ourselves either saying this or being reminded of how true it is. In a sense a lot of the things we've talked about so far (Principle 2, "Know what you're trying to do," Principle 3, "There is always a sequence of events," and Principle 4, "Things don't get done if people don't do them") have been about trying to reduce the likelihood of these surprises happening. Some of the main tools described, especially dance cards and strip boards, are about looking into the future and probing for surprises.

Despite your best efforts, however, there will always be surprises out there waiting. If you don't actively attack the risks on your project, says software authority Tom Gilb, the risks will actively attack you [1]. Sometimes I think we are like people walking through minefields. The tools already described give us partial maps of the minefield, but we know that these maps are partial and that unknown mines still lie there waiting for us.

To deal with these mines, you need some tools. The first tool is the use of contingency, padding, or margin for error. This tool is the equivalent of wearing body armor as you pass through the minefield. You know the mines are there, you assume that it is going to be impossible to avoid stepping on some of them, so you realize that some of them will definitely explode. What you want to ensure then is that the inevitable explosions don't kill you. This is not a stupid approach: Not dying is a very laudable and worthwhile aim! Contingency is a reactive thing. When a surprise occurs, the contingency (hopefully) enables you to deal with it.

However, you can also do a smarter thing: Look out over the minefield and identify suspicious-looking bumps in the ground or signs of digging that indicate there is a fair likelihood that a mine is in place. Then, as you progress through the minefield, you can try to manage your progress as best you can to get past those particular mines. These mines might still go off, and then the body armor contingency is there to save your bacon. You might also have taken specific additional measures to deal with specific mines. If the mines don't go off, then so much the better—your efforts will be repaid many times over in terms of the number of fires you don't have to put out. This latter approach is called risk management.

These two tools—the use of contingency and risk management—are described in the next "Tools" section.

Tools

Contingency

It's possible to make this whole discussion reasonably complicated. Bearing in mind Principle 1 (" Many things are simple"), let's see if we can avoid doing that. Therefore, rather than trying to get into an exhaustive discussion of contingency, let's converge quickly on a few simple ideas.

The first is that it's mandatory. It's not that you'll only have it on your more cushy undertakings and jettison it on those that are down to the wire. You must have it on every venture. (If you remain unconvinced of this, go back to Question 1 at the start of this chapter.)

Now, in mature industries, such as construction or manufacturing or filmmaking, contingency is a fact of life the same way that raw materials or labor rates are facts of life. Unfortunately, the same cannot be said of many of the current high-tech or knowledge industries. Here contingency tends to be viewed with the same kind of suspicion and loathing normally afforded to chewing gum on somebody's shoe: suspicion because somehow it's felt that the people asking for the contingency are going to use it to take a paid holiday, and loathing because it's seen as a way for people to take the easy way out, "remove the creative tension," make things comfortable for themselves, or be cowards.

As a result of this bizarre view, the general tendency in such industries is to remove contingency whenever it's sighted. Given that we have already said that you must have contingency in the plan, then you need to be aware of this tendency and counteract it when it arises. There are two ways to do this:

- Put contingency explicitly into the plan and stop anyone from taking it out.

- Hide it in the plan so that they can't find it.

There's actually a third option, which is to do both these things and let them take the explicit contingency out. Then they have the satisfaction of taking it out, and you still have it. Of course, if you managed to stop them from taking it out, then you would have twice as much and you wouldn't hear any arguments from me on that score.

Finally, how do you do it? Well, here are two good ways (as I said earlier, they're not the only ones, but this isn't an exhaustive discussion):

- Promise less and deliver more. (This is the "have to have" versus the "nice to have" that we raised in the question at the start of the chapter.)

- Pad the estimates, say, of budgets (i.e., make the budget bigger than you think you'll need), resources needed (say you'll need more than you actually need, or say you want to hold on to them for longer), or time needed (i.e., add extra time onto the project).

Risk Management

As we've covered already, many things are simple. Although there are many complicated approaches to risk management, here's a simple one that gets the job done. First of all, it identifies the issues and then gives you a way of dealing with them over the life of the venture.

To manage risks you need to know a few things about them. Specifically, you need to know the following:

- The risks likely to affect your undertaking

- The likelihood of each of those risks to happen

- The impact of each of those risks

- A calculation of your exposure to each risk so that you can deal with the major exposures

- Action(s) you can take to reduce exposures

- Indicators, which will enable you to see if a particular risk has begun to materialize

Use the table shown in Figure 5.1 to record all this.

Risk	Likelihood	Impact	Exposure	Actions	Indicators
	1 = Low 2 = Medium 3 = High	1 = Low 2 = Medium 3 = High	Likelihood × Impact (1 to 9)		

Figure 5.1 Risk management form.

Using Figure 5.1 enables you to see the main risks of your venture. (Risks with an exposure rating of 9 will be the ones you should focus on first.) Then, on an ongoing basis, you can update Figure 5.1 to give you a "Top 10 Risks" list. Focusing regularly (for example, weekly) on these will ensure that you stay on top of the scary things as your venture unfolds.

Examples

Example 22: Getting Your Way with the Boss

Before we start to use the tools just described, I need to remind you of a very simple way to create contingency or backup plans, using a tool introduced in an earlier chapter. You might remember that in Chapter 3 we talked about sequences of events and about how there always had to be another way. If you think about it, this is a backup plan, isn't it?

Let's say, for example, there's somebody who works for you and you want to give him or her a salary raise. Unfortunately, it's not just your decision. You have to convince your boss that this is a good thing to do. Rather than having just one course of action, you might decide that you will have a whole series of possible approaches and you will play each one if the preceding one doesn't work. This might be particularly true if you had already intimated to the favored employee that he or she was going to get a raise. If that's the case, then you really can't afford to fail, and so having backup plans is even more important. So you might try this:

1. Have a conversation with the boss extolling the employee's virtues and explaining how underpaid he or she is. Maybe, without you saying anything, the boss will spontaneously propose that the employee get a raise. A bit unlikely? The worst case is that you've managed to get the item on the table and alerted the boss to the fact that this is on your agenda.

2. On a separate occasion, ask the boss outright. If he or she agrees, you're home. If not, go to Step 3.

3. Gather competitive salary information showing that, for the kind of job the employee does, he or she is underpaid. If the boss agrees, you're home. If not, go to Step 4.

4. Seek a promotion for the employee on the basis that this seems to be the only way he or she can get recognition. If the boss agrees, you're home. If not, go to Step 5.

5. Propose to your boss that if he or she didn't want to raise the employee's salary, there might be other ways of reward—perhaps vouchers or some sort of car allowance or something like that. If the boss agrees, you're home. If not, go to Step 6.

6. Propose to your boss that the employee gets some kind of bonus or ex gratia payment. It's not the same as a salary raise, but it's better than nothing.

I probably don't need to go on here. If you want more ideas, brainstorm (see Chapter 3) with a colleague for half an hour. Try to come up with 40 or 50 ways to solve this problem. (It's not as hard as you think.) Then pick the ways that you want to try, and try them.

Example 23: Risk Analysis for a Company's Business Plan

Table 5.1 illustrates a risk analysis of a company's business plan. You will see from some of the risks (e.g., the first one) that the people who filled this out were being brutally honest. This obviously makes for the best kind of risk analysis!

Table 5.1 Sample risk analysis.

	Risks	Likelihood	Impact	L × I	Action	Indicators
1	Poor management by company's executives	2	3	6	• Performance review • Training • Quality assurance • Strengthen management team	• Departure from monthly plans/targets
2	Under-resourcing	3	3	9	• Verify targets against market data • Hire more people in January • Sort out dance cards of existing staff	• Departure from monthly plans/targets
3	Staff get sick	2	3	6	• Shadowing • Medicals for new employees • Sort any existing problems	• Increase in monthly days lost due to sick leave
4	Lack of expertise	2	3	6	• Training and development • Proper and timely appraisals	• Things get screwed up
5	Office space blowout	1	1	1	• Begin looking for extra facilities	• People unable to find desks or conference/meeting facilities • Overexpenditure on external facilities
6	Competition	1	2	2	• Continue competitor watch	• New competitors identified
7	Revenues don't happen; forecast is wrong	2	3	6	• Weekly monitoring and change control • Financial and management reports	• Departure from monthly plans/targets
8	Staff leave	1	3	3	• Ensure compensation and benefits are keeping pace with industry • Watch morale	• Staff exits look as though exceeding acceptable attrition rate identified

Table 5.1 Sample risk analysis (*continued*).

Risks	Likelihood	Impact	L × I	Action	Indicators
9 Clients walk	1	3	3	• Renew CRM program • Audits on lost customers	• Increase in complaints • Departure by established customers
10 Unrealistic goals	2	3	6	• Change control	• Departure from monthly plans/targets
11 Data security	3	3	9	• Discuss on Dec. 7 at special meeting	• Hacking • Breaches of firewalls • Theft
12 Brand fatigue	2	2	4	• Get marketing to address and make a proposal	• Await marketing's report
13 Cash flow	2	3	6	• Keep on it	• Departure from monthly plans/targets
14 Market changes	1	3	3	• Marketing to keep watching	• Departure from monthly plans/targets
15 Recession hits	1	3	3	• Run a tight ship—look for waste, unnecessary expenditure, etc.	• Departure from monthly plans/targets
16 New market distracts management	1	3	3	• Stick to plan	• Departure from monthly plans/targets

So What Should You Do?

1. Add contingency into all of your plans using the techniques we described in the "Tools" section.

2. Do risk analyses on all of your plans.

3. Maintain a "Top 10 Risks" list and review it on a regular (weekly, monthly) basis.

PRINCIPLE 1: MANY THINGS ARE SIMPLE

PRINCIPLE 2: KNOW WHAT YOU'RE TRYING TO DO

PRINCIPLE 3: THERE IS ALWAYS A SEQUENCE OF EVENTS

PRINCIPLE 4: THINGS DON'T GET DONE IF PEOPLE DON'T DO THEM

PRINCIPLE 5: THINGS RARELY TURN OUT AS EXPECTED

References

1. Gilb, Tom, *Principles of Software Engineering Management*, Addison-Wesley, 1988.

6

THINGS EITHER ARE
OR THEY AREN'T

How do you know if you're making progress toward your objective?
Because things either are or they aren't; things either are done or
they're not. This chapter describes how to know the difference.

Questions

1. An employee is working on a task for you. You ask him how it's going. He says, "I'm 90 percent done." What does this mean?

    (a) He had 100 widgets to process and he has processed 90 of them; therefore 10 remain to be done.

    (b) He's done a whole bunch of work over the last few days.

    (c) He had 10 days to do the task and this is the ninth one. Therefore, he must be 90 percent done.

    (d) The deadline is approaching fast and he wants to make both you and himself feel good.

2. Things are running according to plan. However, you have a vague feeling that morale is not good and that it's only a matter of time before everything goes horribly wrong. What's your best response to this situation?

    (a) Do nothing. If things are going according to plan, then that's all you need to know.

    (b) Begin some morale-boosting activities—the usual suspects: t-shirts, nights out, and so on.

    (c) Publicize how well things are going and how all of the team are pulling together to make the plan happen.

    (d) Investigate why you think there might be morale problems and what these might be.

3. You are part of a project. You finish a job several days early. If it turned out that your job was on the critical path (i.e., was on the shortest path through the project) then the project could be shortened by the same number of days. You go to the project manager and tell him or her. What is most likely to happen to the gift of several days that you hand the project manager?

(a) It depends on whether it's on the critical path. If it is, the project manager will use it wisely to shorten the project. If not it'll just get frittered away.

(b) The project manager will give you something else to do to fill the several days.

(c) Nothing. It'll just get frittered away.

(d) You don't care. It's not your problem.

Answers

1. (a) 5 points

Yes, this could indeed be true. However, in most knowledge and high-tech industries, things are rarely as clear cut as this.

(b) 0 points

I'm sure he has. How that might lead him to believe he is 90 percent done is not clear to me.

(c) 0 points

One of the great illusions of all time. The amount of time the employee has expended on this task might actually bear no relation to the amount of progress he has made. (Read the preceding again if you gave this answer.)

(d) 0 points

I'm sure it is and I'm sure he does. The worrying thing is that in many cases, he'll succeed (in making you feel good, I mean).

2. (a) 4 points

I've given you most of the points, but I'd just have that worry that there might be something afoot.

(b) 3 points

I've given you one less point than the preceding answer on the basis that if this is all you do, and there is a morale problem, blindly doing this won't necessarily fix it.

(c) 4 points

If there is a problem with morale, this *might* help to improve it. Keeping people in touch with how plans are progressing certainly can't hurt.

(d) 5 points

Of course, you'd be far better off trying to find what the problem—if there is one—is in the first place.

3. (a) 0 points

In my experience this is generally *not* what happens. However, using it wisely is what *should* happen.

(b) 5 points

This will almost always happen! However, if the project manager's only interest was to ensure that you had something to keep you busy, then he or she missed the point totally.

(c) 5 points

In my experience, this is what is most likely to happen.

(d) 0 points

Technically, this might be true. However, you should care about the problem.

Scores

14–15 points   You have a wonderfully realistic view of the world.

5–13 points   These are deceptively tricky questions, in my view.

Less than 5 points   You didn't really get any right. Try them again, thinking carefully about the answers.

The Idea

The ideas we've talked about so far (Principle 2, "Know what you're trying to do," Principle 3, "There is always a sequence of events," and Principle 4, "Things don't get done if people don't do them") provide a framework for getting things done. Principle 5, "Things rarely turn out as expected," points out that things will almost certainly turn out differently from the way Principles 2 through 4 might have led us to believe. Given that this is so, we need a way of finding out how things are actually progressing.

Again, the textbooks have no shortages of ways to help us—percentage complete, earned value, milestones passed, number of tasks complete, percentage of budget expended. The list is endless. For exponents of common sense, there is a measure that comes much closer to the core of the problem. That measure is to say that once we have our sequence of events and once we know who's doing what, then each job on the sequence of events can only exist in one of two states. Either it's done or—failing that—it's not done.

Now you might immediately raise an obvious objection to this. That is to say that you might be somewhere in the middle of something and that this is a more useful measure than to say it's not done. I would certainly agree with this. However, to say that you're in the middle of something is really not all that useful either. You should be able to do better than simply saying, "I'm in the middle of something."

Once again, the trick is to break things down and, as we saw in Chapter 3, to do it in as much detail as possible. If you're working on a two-month job, and you tell me you're halfway through, then, in almost all cases, this means almost nothing. However, if the two-month job can be thought of as being composed of, say, 10 or 15 smaller jobs, each of three or four days' duration, then you now actually tell me a great deal of useful information.

If the first month is over and you tell me you're still working on job 1 out of 15, then clearly there's a problem. Equally, if one month is over and tell me that jobs 1 through 7 are done and you're now working on job 8, this tells an entirely different story. So, too, would telling me that after one month, only 1 job out of 15 remains to be done.

Because—hopefully—you will have already built your sequence of events in as much detail as possible, then it should be no great hardship to monitor progress in this way. Of course, if you don't put in this kind of detail, then the job becomes something of a black box, where you have no clear idea what's going on inside. It's out of this lack of clarity that surprises and firefights are born. With black box jobs, you have no real early warning system.

Another issue here is determining what constitutes being done. Here we can use Principle 2 ("Know what you're trying to do") to help us. In the same way that it is important to know for large projects or strategies precisely what it is you're trying to achieve, it is also important to know this for each of the jobs in your sequence of events. Each job should produce some deliverable, some thing that you can look at or hold in your hand, and verify that the existence of this thing means that this job is done.

Tools

How Are We Doing?

The first of our tools is the one I hinted at in the opening section. When assessing progress, we will think not in terms of partway through or 60 percent done or any of these vague notions. Rather, we will break a job down into elements (smaller jobs), and we will then record those jobs as being either done or not done. If somebody tries anything else, then we will not allow that, but rather ask that person to break the thing down into jobs that he or she can then classify as either done or not done.

At first, people might find this notion a bit alien and you might have to coach them into understanding what you mean, what you want, and why what you're asking for might actually make sense. I think you'll also find people incentivized to break things down into smaller units of detail because of the following effect. Say you have weekly meetings to assess status. Somebody won't want to attend week after week, while still reporting that the same large task is not done. Instead, if the task is broken down into smaller components, some progress can actually be reported from week to week.

Are Things Better or Worse?

A variant on the notion of things either are or they aren't is the idea that things are better or worse. Things either are or they aren't is an instantaneous snapshot of the status of something. However, we might be interested in how the status of something is progressing over time. Let's say, for example, you run a company and it's experiencing cash flow difficulties. You are anxious to know some key indicators:

- Are costs decreasing?
- Are revenues increasing?
- What's happening to profits?
- How far are you on your lines of credit?

Asking whether things are better or worse, from day to day, week to week, or month to month will help clarify for you what the trends are. Graphing the answer to the question will make all of this abundantly clear.

Examples

Example 24: Monitoring Progress

We already looked at the idea of breaking things down and then reporting the smaller jobs identified as being either done or not done. There
is an additional aspect of this that is worth noting. Say, for example,
you have a weekly status meeting where people must say how they're
doing. (These comments apply equally well when the status is reported via progress reports rather than a meeting.) If someone is attending
week after week and reporting that a particular job they're working on
is not done, then the (peer or self-imposed) pressure generated by this
should cause that person to focus more on getting the thing done, so
that he or she can report that it's finished.

Example 25: Reducing Stress (Part 1)

You can use Principle 6 and Principle 3 ("There is always a sequence
of events") to help you reduce stress. In Chapter 3, you saw the idea of
thinking of the sequence of events as a stack from which we took jobs
as they needed to be done. In considering each of these jobs, we can
determine—using Principle 6—if it must be done by us or not. If we
must do it, then let's get to it. If not, then that should mean somebody
else must do it. In that case, there is nothing you can do about it, and
there's no point in worrying about it, so just wait until they get it done.
The Dalai Lama puts it succinctly in saying that if a situation or problem is such that it cannot be fixed, there is no need to worry about it—
you can't do anything about it anyway [1].

There is a variation on this that makes it even more watertight.
When you've identified that the next move is not yours, ask yourself
one additional question: Is there anything you can do to expedite the
next job, even though it is not yours? If there is, this becomes a job in
your stack. That being the case, go do it. If, however, there is genuine-

ly nothing further you can do, you're off the hook until the next person get his or her bit done.

Example 26: Reducing Stress (Part 2)

You can also use identifying whether things are getting better or worse to reduce stress. By checking whether things are better or worse than they were, you can establish whether things have bottomed out. Are things going downhill or have they turned around and are now starting to improve?

Example 27: Problem Solving Revisited

The "are things better or worse" tool provides us with a useful way of generating potential solutions to problems. We can start out by asking, "What would be the simplest possible solution to this problem?" Then, if it is our feeling that this solution might not be viable, for whatever reason, we can look for the next most complicated one by changing one of the variables involved in the problem. This generates a new, somewhat more complicated solution. We can continue doing this until we have generated a number of solutions, ranging from the simplest to the most complicated. Then we can reach in and pick the one that is most appropriate to our needs.

So What Should You Do?

1. Monitor progress on the basis of things being done or not done. Break things down to a lower level of detail where necessary.

> PRINCIPLE 1: MANY THINGS ARE SIMPLE
>
> PRINCIPLE 2: KNOW WHAT YOU'RE TRYING TO DO
>
> PRINCIPLE 3: THERE IS ALWAYS A SEQUENCE OF EVENTS
>
> PRINCIPLE 4: THINGS DON'T GET DONE IF PEOPLE DON'T DO THEM
>
> PRINCIPLE 5: THINGS RARELY TURN OUT AS EXPECTED
>
> PRINCIPLE 6: THINGS EITHER ARE OR THEY AREN'T

References

1. His Holiness The Dalai Lama and Cutler, Howard C., *The Art of Happiness*, New York: Riverhead Books, 1998, p. 268.

7

LOOK AT THINGS FROM OTHERS' POINTS OF VIEW

In Chapter 1, we talked of seeing things simply. One simple way of seeing things is to see them from other people's points of view. Almost everything we undertake involves other people. Seeing things as they see them can be a powerful aid to understanding and getting things done.

Questions

1. You've joined a new organization and you've discovered that one of the people who works for you appears to be seriously overpaid for what he does. You know that he is pretty settled and happy in the organization. You also know that he's fairly reasonable. You decide to reduce his salary to that of his peers. Your analysis is that although he might be very upset about it initially, he will eventually see your point of view and the whole thing will blow over. Is this what actually happens?

   (a) Yes, it's all about how settled and happy he is in the organization—that plus the fact that he's a reasonable person.

   (b) He goes ballistic. He quits and you end up with a lawsuit on your hands.

   (c) It's stormier than you had expected. You have to give a bit and not do as big a reduction as you had been planning. Then it passes.

   (d) You sleep on it, wake up the next day, and decide this was a crazy idea. You've got plenty on your plate without bringing this on yourself. You let sleeping dogs lie.

2. You join an organization where your boss weilds a need-to-know policy. He will tell you the minimum you need to know to get the job done. Your style is very much the opposite. Your approach is to tell everybody the big picture and their part in it. You consider converting your boss to your approach as one of your big crusades, but you're not sure how important it is, given all the other things you have on your plate. How important is it?

   (a) High priority.

   (b) Medium priority.

   (c) Low priority.

   (d) Irrelevant (i.e., no priority) in the sense that it's just the way things are and you'll have to work within these parameters.

3. Of the following, which is the worst crime?

(a) Telling bad news to the higher ups.

(b) Telling good news to the higher ups.

(c) Telling no news to the higher ups.

(d) Giving the higher ups (bad) surprises.

Answers

1. (a) 0 points

Reasonable or not, I couldn't see this happening in a month of Sundays.

(b) 5 points

He quits? Almost certainly. A lawsuit? You can depend on it. And he'd win, too. The payout would dwarf the saving you would have made by reducing his salary.

(c) 0 points

Most unlikely, I'd say. Reducing somebody's salary strikes at a fundamental core of their being.

(d) 5 points

I'd like to think this is what you chose.

2. (a) 5 points

In my view, absolutely. Not dealing with this essentially commits the organization to an active policy of ignoring how people feel about things.

(b) 1 point

Your heart's in the right place.

(c) 0 points

See (a).

(d) 0 points

See (a).

3. (a) 5 points

This is not a crime (although, in many organizations it is treated as such). Ultimately, people don't expect miracles (although again, I realize you might be saying that in your organization, they do). What people really want is that good, bad, or indifferent, they know how they stand. In this context, telling bad news is the right thing to do.

(b) 4 points

Provided it's the truth, this is not a crime. I've docked a point—unfairly, you might cry—to remind you of this painful fact.

(c) 4 points

Provided there's nothing to report, this is not a crime. If there is and you're hiding it or sitting on it, then you're being very naughty indeed. I've docked a point as a reminder, as before.

(d) 5 points

This is a crime.

Scores

15 points   This is a very good score here and shows a strong sensitivity to these types of issues.

14 points   Yes, not bad.

Less than 14 points   These types of things are too important to get wrong.

The Idea

This final principle is a very old one. Interestingly, it is also common to a number of the world's major religions. For example, you might know of the Talmud, the 20-volume work that can be thought of as an encyclopedia of Judaism. The Talmud tells the story of a Gentile who comes to a rabbi and asks to be taught all of Judaism while standing on one foot. One of the rabbi's students has the man driven from the rabbi's door, taking the question to be impertinent or mocking. Unperturbed, the rabbi replies, "What is offensive to you, do not do to others. That is the core of Judaism. The rest is commentary. Now carry on your studies" [1].

Buddhism also has a view on this principle. The Dalai Lama says that empathy is important not only as a means of enhancing compassion, but that when you're having trouble dealing with others, it's extremely helpful to be able to try to put yourself in the other person's place and see how you would react to the same situation [2]. Finally, the notion of "do as you would be done to" is widely known in the Christian faith.

The six principles we have seen so far are very much about getting things done. More than anything else, the thing that will determine how easy or difficult things are to get done will be how people react to them. If people are positive and well motivated, they will move mountains. On the other hand, if people are not well disposed toward what is being attempted, in an extreme case, they will bring it to a halt.

The idea then, is very simple: See things from other people's viewpoints and modify your plans and behavior, if necessary, to maximize your chances of success. Precisely how you do this is the subject of the next section.

Tools

Put Yourself in Their Shoes

Once again, the Dalai Lama describes this technique very simply by saying that you must have the capacity to temporarily suspend your viewpoint and look at the situation from the other person's perspective.

Imagine what would be the situation if you were in the other person's place. This helps you develop an awareness and respect for another's feelings, which is an important factor in reducing conflicts and problems with other people [3].

My editor, Rachael Stock, put it another way, but no less eloquently, by saying, "Never assume you know everything." Or, to put it yet another way, "Be open to learning from others." Finally, the point is also made by Stephen Covey in his best-selling *The Seven Habits of Highly Effective People* [4]. One of Covey's seven habits is to think win/win.

Maximize the Win Conditions of the Stakeholders

We saw this concept already in Chapter 2, when we looked at the "know if what you're trying to do is what everyone wants" tool. Just to remind you, the stakeholders are all of those people affected by what you're intending to do. Each of those stakeholders will have a set of win conditions. Win conditions are those things that they want to get from the particular venture or undertaking. It is quite likely that the various win conditions will not be compatible with one another. Anyone who has even a passing acquaintance with the peace talks in Northern Ireland or the Middle East should have no problem understanding this concept. Given that the various win conditions are often more or less incompatible, this tool is about trying to find a set of win conditions that everyone can live with. You'll remember we described a way of doing this in Chapter 2, Example 4.

Examples

Example 28: Meetings Revisited

Using all of our principles, we can now see how to conduct a decent meeting. We can also use our principles to spot when we've been saddled with a turkey—a meeting that will consume everybody's time and be of little or no value.

To conduct a meeting you need to do the following:

1. Figure out the objectives of the meeting (Principle 2, "Know what you're trying to do").

2. Identify the things that must get done to get you to the objectives (Principle 3, "There is always a sequence of events").

3. People are going to have to do those things (Principle 4, "Things don't get done if people don't do them"). Thus, Principles 2 and 4 identify who has to come to the meeting.

4. Principles 2 and 4 also enable us to build the agenda, including a time constraint on each agenda item. Using Principle 5 ("Things rarely turn out as expected"), add in some contingency to give a time constraint on the meeting as a whole.

5. Publish the objectives, agenda, and time constraints, and indicate to each participant what preparation, if any, is required from him or her (Principle 7, "Look at things from others' points of view").

6. Hold the meeting, guiding it by the agenda and time constraints you identified (Principle 4, "Things don't get done if people don't do them").

7. Prepare an action list arising from the meeting (Principle 3, "There is always a sequence of events").

8. Stop when the time is up. By then, if you've done your job properly, the objectives should have been met.

To spot a turkey, when you are asked to come to a meeting, ask these questions:

- What is the objective?

- Why do you need to go? In other words, what leads them to believe that you can contribute anything useful?

- What preparation do you have to do?

- How long will it last?

If you can't get sensible answers to all of these questions, then you're probably onto a loser. For your best bet in those circumstances, see Question 1 at the beginning of Chapter 2.

Example 29: Doing the Right Project

Projects are hot these days, I think you'll agree. Everyone is suddenly using the language of project management: deadline, milestone, Gantt chart, and so on. People generally start (or should start) projects because of some business benefit that will accrue from them. Being clear about the business benefit enables you to launch the right project. Being unclear results in projects that invariably chew up time, money, and resources, and make a number of people unhappy.

We have seen the two principles that will enable us to launch the right project (Principle 2, "Know what you're trying to do," and Principle 7, "Look at things from others' points of view"). Knowing what we're trying to do enables us to identify the type of project we want to do. Looking at things from the points of view of the other stakeholders enables us to pick precisely the version of the project that is right for us. Again, look at Example 4 in Chapter 2 for more on this.

Example 30: Status Reporting

In status reporting there seem to be two schools of thought: Tell them nothing or tell them everything. Interestingly, both schools have something in common. Both types of reports can result in you not getting any information at all on the status of things. In the first case, this is because they didn't actually give you any, whereas in the second, it's because they overwhelmed you with so much information that it's impossible to see the forest for the trees. Principle 7 tells us that we have to tell others what we're doing. It doesn't say we must tell everybody 100 percent of everything, but it does say that we can't tell them nothing.

Now, if we're not going to tell everybody 100 percent of everything, what are we going to do? Well, we must filter what we're saying in some way, but not so much that the message is garbled, misunderstood, hidden, or reversed. In my experience, the majority of traditional status reports, whether written or verbal, do all of these things. In general, such status reports have the following feel about them: They give the impression that there are impressive amounts of work happening—we did this, we did that, this happened, that happened. (The message is, "We're earning our money.") Not everything that happens is good, so status reports are always keen to report bad incidents. (The message is, "We're *really* earning our money.") However, there's always the almost compulsory happy ending, the feeling that in spite of everything, we're going to be okay. In other words, few status reports are prepared to report bad news.

In general, people are interested in one or more of the following aspects of what you're doing:

- Will I get everything I thought I was going to get and if not, what can I expect?

- Is it on time, and if not what can I now expect?

- How's it doing on costs? Over? Under? About right?

- Will the thing I get meet my needs?

In reporting the status, you need to tell them about which of these things they are interested in. You also need to tell them both the instantaneous status—here's how it is today—and what the status is over time—in other words, the trend. Only then can they have a true picture of how things are going. By knowing the trend, they can understand not just the kind of shape we're in today, but how things might unfold in the future, so there are no surprises in store for anybody.

Finally, whom are we talking about here? All of the stakeholders, as defined earlier. In general, there are at least four that we can always regard as being present. The first is you, the person responsible for getting the thing done; next is your team, the people who are doing the work; third is the customer for whom the work is being done; and finally, there is your boss. All of these need to be given an insight—not necessarily the same one—into how things are proceeding.

First you need to understand that status yourself. Principle 6 ("Things either are or they aren't") will aid you in doing this. Once you know, by considering the status from other people's points of view (Principle 7, "Look at things from others' points of view"), you can deliver the status to them. It will be a message that they can understand (because it is expressed in terms that are real to them), that gives the status (because it tells the truth), and that seeks to clarify rather than obscure how things are going.

Figure 7.1 gives an example of some extracts from a status report that illustrate both instantaneous status and one possible trend we might be interested in.

Example 31: Marketing Revisited

Marketing is all about seeing what you are selling from the potential customer's point of view. Essentially, it's very simple: Your potential customer must have one or more problems that you can solve. Usually, these problems revolve around one of three things—making more money, gaining market edge, or making life easier for themselves. If you can put yourself in their shoes (through surveys, information gathering by your sales force, or whatever), you can understand the problems they have under each of these headings. If you can then see how what you sell addresses these problems, you are well on your way to making more money and gaining market edge yourself.

STATUS REPORT

Project:	*Great Product Version 1.2*
Report:	*14*
Date:	*October, 21 2003*
Project Manager:	Frank
Team:	Rachel, Debbie, Declan, Steve, Mary
Distribution:	As above plus Bernadette, Hugh, Dan, Pedro, Ted, File + Tell anyone else who's interested

Overall Status:

Requirements	Design	Development	Testing	Limited Customer Release
Complete	Complete	Complete	In progress	Not yet started

Current dates are:
  Testing to complete on November 17, 2003.
  General availability (at end of limited customer release) January 19, 2004.

Trends

Delivery Date—change history

Date of Change	Reason for Change	Into Beta Date	General Availability Date
	Original dates	May 1, 2003	Sep 1, 2002
May 9, 2003	See section 1 of the Project Plan	Nov 24, 2003	Jan 23, 2004
May 27, 2003	Added an extra person for a few weeks	Nov 12, 2003	Jan 12, 2004
July 2, 2003	Some improvements due to use of Mary	Nov 3, 2003	Jan 5, 2004
Oct 14, 2003	Slip in development schedule	Nov 17, 2003	Jan 19, 2004

Figure 7.1 Status report.

Example 32: Planning and Executing a Project

If you are asked to plan and execute a project—a project to do pretty much anything—then you essentially bring into play almost all of our seven principles. When a project is handed to you, you've actually been handed two things: One is the request itself and the other is something that I often think of as the *baggage* or *fixed constraints*. The baggage or fixed constraints relates to the idea that when people are handing over a project, they will generally say that it must be done by such and such a date, or for this budget, or with these resources.

If you try to process the request and the baggage together, you will get yourself into a lot of trouble, because in processing the request, you will be thinking of all the time you're going to need, all the resources, the budget, and so on. The baggage will be telling you that you don't have the time, you won't get the budget, and the vast army of people you're going to need is probably going to end up being one man and a dog.

The thing to do then is to deal with the request and the baggage separately. First, understand the request, then use what you have learned to make sensible decisions about the baggage. Our principles of common sense enable you to do precisely this.

Let's assume that the request and baggage have arrived. Put the baggage to one side for the present and focus on the request. Principle 2 states, "Know what you're trying to do." What precisely is this project about? What is it not about? The "understanding what you're trying to do" tool in Chapter 2 enables you to do this. In addition, if you use Principle 7 ("Look at things from others' points of view"), you can maximize the win conditions of the stakeholders; that is, you can ensure that the outcome of the project is the best possible outcome from the point of view of all people involved.

Next, use Principle 3 ("There is always a sequence of events") to understand what has to be done to achieve the result you have identified. After that, Principle 4 ("Things don't get done if people don't do them") forces you to make sure that every job in the sequence of events has a person or people to do it, and that people have sufficient time available to work on this particular thing. (Dance cards are the tool to use for this.) You can also look at maximizing the strengths of the team as described in Chapter 4. Principle 5 ("Things rarely turn out as expected") allows you to put contingency or margin for error into your plans.

At this point we have properly analyzed the request that we have been given. We have the clearest picture available of how the project could unfold. (Note that we could have represented this picture in a number of different ways. It could be represented as a Gantt chart—a who-does-what-when representation; a spreadsheet—a who-spends-what-when and who-earns-what-when representation; a strip board as described in Chapter 4, or in other ways.) Now we can go deal with the baggage.

In general, then, what the plan says can happen and what the baggage says needs to happen are not the same thing. People usually then throw away the plan and accept the baggage. By this action they are implicitly saying that the plan is wrong, despite the fact that the plan represents the best guess anyone has for this project.

Our principles tell us that this is precisely the wrong thing to do. Principle 6 ("Things either are or they aren't") tells us that if the plan isn't the same as the baggage, no amount of wishing will make it so, and neither will ignoring unpleasant facts. The correct thing to do is to say that the plan represents our best shot at this project; knowing this, what can we do about the baggage? Can we add more people or money or other resources? Can we reduce the scope of what we intended to do? Is the level of quality we were looking at still required or can we get by with something less? We do this until the plan and the baggage meet, or until we get to a realistic plan that those who brought the baggage can live with.

Then, coming back again to Principle 7 ("Look at things from others' points of view"), we tell everybody involved in the project the plan and their part in it. Now we're ready to begin the project and we have defined a game that we have some chance of winning, whereas, if we had blithely accepted the baggage, in many cases, the game would already be lost—all that remains is for it to be played out.

To run the project, we execute the plan we have developed. Principle 6 ("Things either are or they aren't") tells us how we are proceeding. Principle 1 ("Know what you're trying to do") ensures that we stay aware of the changes in the scope of the project that can occur during its lifetime. (In general, these are new things being added for a variety of reasons; e.g., they were forgotten initially, what we thought we wanted wasn't what we really wanted, the business need has changed, the market has changed, there has been some change in technology, we've found a better way to do something, we estimated something as being much smaller or bigger than it actually turned out to be, and so on.) Once again, Principle 7 ("Look at things from others' points of view") ensures that we report progress in a meaningful way to all of the stakeholders.

Finally, when the project ends we will want to spend some time doing a postmortem, recording what actually happened so that the process of planning the next project can be made easier. We discussed this in Chapter 3.

Example 33: Common-Sense Time Management

There was a theory going around about 10 years ago that said that in a few years' time, we'd have all this leisure time that we wouldn't know what to do with. The notion was that with all the various labor-saving devices around (especially computers and computer-driven devices) much of our day-to-day drudgery would be taken away from us. The concern then was about educating people for leisure. You don't hear much about that any more. Try telling it to, say, an urban couple who get up at some ungodly hour, wash, eat, ferry children to a number of different schools or to day care, join the traffic jam for work, work an eight-hour (if they're lucky) day, and then do it all in reverse that evening.

As an aside, it seems to me there was a basic flaw in this and a number of other assumptions that have been made about modern society. Principle 1 ("Many things are simple") enables us to spot this flaw without much difficulty, and it is best illustrated by an example. You might remember the notion of the paperless office that was fashionable during the 1980s. The idea was that you would give people computers with plenty of disk storage, high-speed printers, copiers, and electronic links, and the result would be the disappearance of filing cabinets and paper. Everything would be available online. Now thinking simply about this, the notion is ludicrous. If you give people the ability (using computers, networks, printers, and copiers) to generate and pass around large amounts of paper, what will they do? They'll generate and pass around large amounts of paper.

We can see the same effect with traffic. If you give people the ability to do a lot more driving, by building lots of cars and more roadways, what will people do? They'll drive more cars and fill more roadways. Returning to the notion of time management and leisure time, if you give people the ability to communicate more or less instantaneously, what will happen? People will use that ability to try to run their jobs or their businesses faster. They will try to get more done more quickly. Will this have a relaxing effect? You could hardly call getting more done more quickly a recipe for relaxation, could you?

Anyway, back to the main point of common-sense time management. If there is only one thing that I'd like you to take away from this book, it's the notion that you can't, mustn't, and shouldn't allow your time to be stolen from you by other people. There are (I presume) things you are trying to do with your life and your career. The only way you can ensure that these things get done is by giving them their fair share of time. Unless you do this, these things will never happen and your life or career will end up not being the one you wanted. The principles we have seen enable us to build a common-sense time management framework that has two parts to it. First, figure out what you're trying to do, then do it. The doing we will break down into yearly, monthly (or weekly), and daily things. Let's go through it, using some of the tools we have already encountered.

1. **Figure out what you trying to do.**

    We've already seen this in Example 6 of Chapter 2. If you go through the exercise described in Example 6, you will end up with a series of things that you want to do. Ideally, these things should cover the full spread of what you want to do with your life, not just your career or business.

2. **Do it—the annual bit.**

    At the beginning of each new year (or any time that you want to start taking control of your life), lay out the things you want to do on a prioritized dance card as shown in Figure 4.5. To do this, you will have to estimate the work involved in each of the things you're trying to do. We covered how to do this in Chapter 3, Example 8.

    Now, if the dance card shows that there is more work for you to do than there is time available to do it, you must use the ideas we talked about in Examples 15 and 16 in Chapter 4 to balance the dance card. That is to say, you must get the work to be done and the time available to do it into realistic proximity of each other. By *realistic* I mean two things: First, don't jettison things like family time to make extra work time available. Second, don't implicitly or explicitly accept a situation where you are monstrously overloaded. (Remember, a 60 percent overload situation—which is what we saw in Figure 4.5—means that you will have to work an additional 24 hours a week to get everything done.)

3. Do it—the monthly (or weekly) bit.

By doing the estimating we just mentioned, you will have figured out how much work is involved in each of the things you're trying to do. The other result of the estimating will be that each of those things will have a sequence of events (or stack) associated with it. In addition, if you've done the balancing of the dance card, then everything you're trying to do is actually doable (i.e., there is adequate time to do it). If this is not the case, if you are hopelessly overloaded, then there is really not much point in continuing with all of this.

Now, extract from each of the stacks what has to get done this month (or week). Enter this into your diary, organizer, Palm Pilot, Microsoft Outlook, or whatever you use to manage your time. You could also enter it into a dance card that was denominated in weeks or days rather than months. Also, while we're on the subject, the proliferation of things like diaries, organizers, palmtops, and PCs means that sometimes people end up keeping their diary in several places. *Please* don't. Keep it in one place and stick to it! By "enter it," I mean show on which days each of the items from the stack will be done. Again note that the balancing of the annual dance card will ensure that there is adequate time for all of these things.

4. Do it—the daily bit.

It is on a day-by-day basis that you will win or lose the battle to ensure that the right things get done. First thing every morning (or even better, last thing the previous evening), look at the page of your diary that represents today. It will contain several things that are contenders to be done. Some of these things will have come from the stacks as described. Some will have come from your inbox, but will have been processed via the regime we described in Example 15. Now mark each of the items with one of the following letters:

- A—Urgent and important, *must* be done today.

- B—It would be nice to get it done today.

- C—I definitely won't get this done today.

- D—Can be delegated.

Now, handle all of the As and Ds and leave the rest. It is as simple as that, but you might have some questions, so let's see if we can anticipate and answer them.

- **What if you have some time left at the end of the day?**

  Well, you could start on the Bs. However, a more cunning thing to do is to flip the page of your diary to tomorrow, go through the priority assignment process and then begin doing tomorrow's As and Ds. This really keeps you focused on the important things.

- **What if you encounter an interruption?**

  Go through the priority assignment again. Also, by having some contingency in your day (see Example 20, Chapter 4) you can ensure that interruptions don't blow your day away.

- **What if the end of the day comes and some of the As aren't done?**

  In that case, they couldn't have been As! Being brutal about what absolutely has to be done today is, in a very real sense, the essence of common-sense time management.

Finally, record where your time actually goes. A dance card is a good tool for doing this—just add some extra columns to take care of it. It will help with your time estimating and planning in the future.

Example 34: More Stress-Management Techniques

1. **Keep a sense of proportion (or, there is always someone worse off than you).**

   This one comes to us courtesy of the "are things better or worse" tool in Chapter 6. In general, no matter how bleak your situation, it is almost certainly true that there is someone in the world worse off than you. Every day thousands of people die of hunger, disease, torture, execution, neglect, abuse, and loneliness. Most of the things we face don't add up to a hill of beans in the context of these problems. The next time you're feeling stressed, pick up the paper or turn on the news. Alternatively, you could read *The House at Pooh Corner* [5]:

   "Hallo, Eeyore," said Christopher Robin, as he opened the door and came out.

   "How are you?"

   "It's snowing still," said Eeyore gloomily.

   "So it is."

   "And freezing."

   "Is it?"

   "Yes," said Eeyore. "However," he said, brightening up a little, "we haven't had an earthquake lately."

2. **See it a year from now.**

   Principle 7 tells us to see things from others' points of view. Imagine yourself a year from now. How will the issue that is causing you so much worry seem a year from now? Will you actually be able to remember it? Visualize it and see if this brings anything new.

3. **The marathon runner.**

I used to run marathons (not very well, I should add). Now I think you'll agree that the notion of running more than 26 miles is ridiculous. It's outrageous. Rather than thinking about all the appalling stuff that lies ahead, marathon runners use—whether they know it or not—Principle 3, "There is always a sequence of events." Don't worry about the stuff that lies way off in the future. Rather, work your way through the next little job in the sequence. In the case of marathon runners, this means make the next telegraph pole, tree, mile marker, or feeding station. Then turn your attention to the next piece of the journey.

4. **Talk to somebody.**

Principle 7 again. Also, as the old saying goes, a problem shared is a problem halved.

Example 35: Assessing Things—Projects and Project Plans

Increasingly, one of the things you might be required to do is assess plans that are being proposed or undertakings that are actually in progress. For example, a subcontractor might be presenting a plan for something that has been outsourced to them, or you could be asked to make a recommendation on a business plan or the proposed funding of a particular venture. The venture might already be in progress and the question is how well it is doing. Often, these things we are being asked to decide on, are highly technical or complex, and we might not be personally familiar with the technicalities or complexities. How then, do we make the right decision? Our principles of common sense can help us chart a way through the mass of data and unearth the nuggets of information we really need.

It seems to me that sometimes people refer to this as gut feel or gut instinct. Gut feel is not a wild stab in the dark; rather, it is a sense or a feeling that the odds are in your favor. The following is a way of trying to assess those odds.

Imagine you are at a presentation about, or reading a report on, or considering some venture that is occurring on the ground. What do you need to look for?

1. Principle 2, "Know what you're trying to do," tells us that somewhere in the tangle of information there had better be some sort of goal or objective to this thing. This goal must have two main characteristics. First, it must be well defined (i.e., it should be possible to tell unambiguously when this goal will have been achieved). There should be no confusion or fuzziness about whether we will have crossed the finish line. For example, confusion among the stakeholders as to what constituted the end would be a classic breach of this requirement. The goal must also be current (i.e., any changes to it that have occurred along the way should have been accumulated and now be part of the final goal).

2. Principle 3, "There is always a sequence of events," says that somewhere we should be able to see the series of activities that brings us through the project from where we are now to the goal. This sequence of events could be represented in many forms, and we have seen some of them already in this book:

   • A Gantt chart—Who does what and when.

   • A strip board—Who does what and when.

   • A spreadsheet—Who spends or earns what, and when.

   The level of detail of the sequence of events must convince us that somebody has analyzed—as best they can—all of the things that need to be done in this project. Pretty, computer-generated, high-level charts don't cut it—unless they can show you the supporting detail.

3. Principle 4, "Things don't get done if people don't do them," mandates that there be someone leading the venture, and all of the jobs in the sequence of events have names assigned to them. Also,

availability should be clear. Names aren't enough. We need to know how much of those people's time is available to work on this venture. Notice that with this step and the preceding one it should be possible to do a very quick calculation that will test the venture to its core. Step 2 should tell you how much work has to be done. This step should tell you how much work is available (i.e., how many people for how much of their time). These two numbers should essentially be the same.

4. Principle 5, "Things rarely turn out as expected," indicates that if the venture has no contingency or margin for error in it, you should send them packing!

Example 36: Seeing Versus Noticing

Example 35 is an example of the more general problem of how to notice the obvious. Perhaps the best way to go about doing this is to use Principle 7 ("Look at things from others' points of view"). For instance, try to imagine what your day—especially your working day—would be like if you were of the opposite sex.

Example 37: Mind Mapping Common Sense

Mind mapping is a powerful tool that can aid learning, problem analysis, and clearer thinking [6]. As the name suggests, mind mapping produces a record in a way that imitates how the human mind works. Thus, words, pictures, colors, and symbols can all form part of a mind map. Although there are some simple conventions for drawing them, mind maps usually end up as individual as the person who produced them.

To draw a mind map, do the following:

- Put the subject under consideration in a central image or picture.

- Make the main ideas associated with that subject radiate from the central image as branches.

- Attach subsidiary ideas to higher-level branches.

Figure 7.2 shows a simple mind map for common sense. The #7 branch has the tools attached as subsidiary ideas.

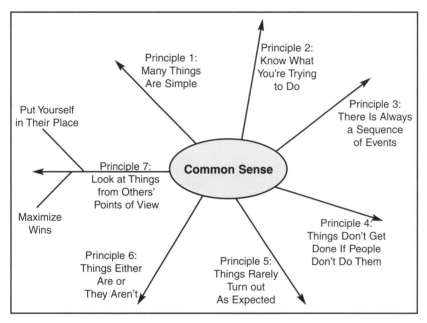

Figure 7.2 A simple mind map for common sense.

I hope you can see that with mind maps you can very quickly generate large amounts of ideas on a given subject. To keep control of and structure these ideas, mind mapping includes the concept of basic ordering ideas (BOIs). Thus, once you've identified the subject you want to consider, the next step is to identify your BOIs, the key concepts within which several other concepts can be organized. To mind map using common sense, I would suggest two possible ways of going about it. One would be to use the simple questions we saw in Chapter 1 as the BOIs (i.e., who, what, why, where, when, how, and which). The other would be to use the principles of common sense themselves. Figure 7.3 does the latter, focusing on the subject of increasing sales.

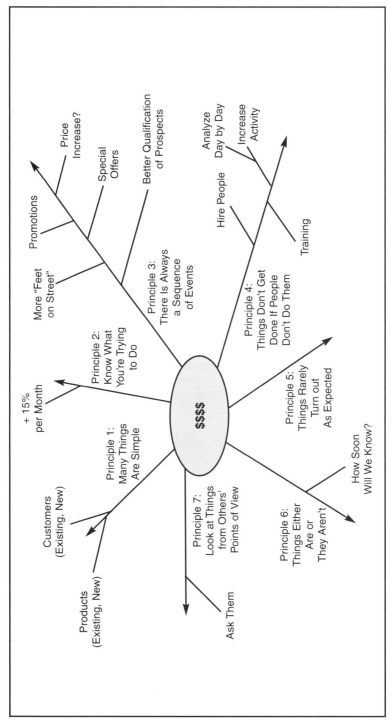

Figure 7.3 The principles of common sense used to increase sales.

Given the large number of ideas that can be generated very quickly using mind mapping, the use of the BOIs we have described provides an effective way to focus common sense on any issue.

Example 38: Gut Feel

Gut feel or trusting your instinct is a skill that seems to be held in very high regard by a certain part of the population and treated with an equal level of disdain by the remainder. Studies at Harvard Business School have shown that senior executives of large national and multinational organizations attributed 80 percent of their success to acting on intuition or gut feel. Other schools of thought seem to regard this as the lazy individual's substitute for proper assembly and analysis of the facts.

What happens when we use our instinct or gut feel to make a decision is this: The brain considers the vast amount of information it has accumulated over our lifetime, along with all of the data related to the current situation. The brain registers an answer to this problem. By *answer*, I mean how likely the proposed course of action is to succeed. This is translated into a biological reaction and this reaction is interpreted by people as their gut feel [7].

By building mind maps as described in Example 37, we give the brain the widest range of information possible on which to make a decision.

Example 39: Build a Fast-Growing Company

In the September 6, 1999, edition of *Fortune* [8], there was an article on America's fastest-growing companies. The article identified seven factors that these companies had in common. Perhaps, at this stage, it should come as no surprise to us that behind these seven factors we can clearly see our principles:

1. The companies always deliver on their commitments. (Principle 7, "Look at things from others' points of view.") If somebody is a

customer of yours then—despite the way it might seem at times—
they don't actually expect miracles. (No, really, it's true!) What
they do expect—and rightly so—is that you will deliver on whatever they have been led to believe, and meet whatever expectations have been set for them.

2. They don't overpromise. (Principle 7, "Look at things from others' points of view" again.) This is really not too different from the
   preceding factor. In the article, this factor was related specifically
   to what companies were promising to deliver—and subsequently
   did deliver—to the financial community and Wall Street.

3. They sweat the small stuff. (Principle 3, "There is always a
   sequence of events.") If you remember, much of what we talked
   about in Chapter 3 was about trying to understand the detail of
   what needed to happen. These days, in many cases, time is an
   even more valuable commodity than money. Knowing where our
   time goes, ensuring that it is spent wisely, removing time wasters,
   and avoiding firefights is what this one is all about.

4. They build a fortress. This one is about protecting your business,
   especially by creating barriers to entry. (Principle 5, "Things
   rarely turn out as expected.") Just because things are going well
   doesn't mean they'll always go well. Maintaining a healthy inse-
   curity about things, always having some contingency in the plan
   and keeping a watchful eye on your Top 10 Risks list will ensure
   that your fortress becomes as impregnable as possible.

5. They create a culture. (Principle 1, "Know what you're trying to
   do.") This factor is about the corporate cultures that these fast-
   growth companies have created. In all of the cases cited, the companies set out to deliberately create a certain kind of culture, be it
   a very formal one, as in the case of Siebel Systems, or an informal
   one, like casual clothes maker American Eagle.

6. They learn from their mistakes. (Principle 3, "There is always a sequence of events" and the tool "record what actually happens.")

7. They shape their story. This, again, is about ensuring that investors and financial analysts never feel uncertain about a company, but rather are kept in the loop by the company about what is going on. Again it's about Principle 7 ("Look at things from others' points of view"). As the article says, "When there is uncertainty with this kind of small, growing company, the first thing people do is run . . . And when one money manager sees someone else bailing out, his first thought is, 'What does that guy know that I don't?' They don't wait around to find out what's really going on" [9].

Example 40: Negotiation

The conventional view of negotiation tends to have a lot to do with arguing until you get your way. Often, you don't necessarily get what you deserve, but rather what you negotiate. Negotiation is something you do to other people, and it has the feel of a bruising contact sport.

A quick dose of Principle 7 ("Look at things from others' points of view") is enough to tell us that this is perhaps not the best way to go about negotiating. There is a great book about negotiating called *Getting to Yes* [10]. Based on work done at Harvard, it describes a four-step approach to negotiation called *principled negotiation* or *negotiation on the merits*. The approach has as its objective to produce a wise agreement, defined to be "one which meets the legitimate interests of each side to the extent possible, resolves conflicting interests fairly, is durable, and takes community interests into account." Rather than taking up positions and arguing, the approach says, "Look, we have this problem—how can we solve it in a way that works for both if us?" In a sense, it's the idea of maximizing the win conditions of the stakeholders that we've already seen. The steps of principled negotiation leap straight out of our common-sense principles:

1. Separate the people from the problem.

2. Focus on interests, not positions.

3. Generate a variety of possibilities before deciding what to do.

4. Insist that the result be based on some objective standard.

Looking through our common sense lens, we could write them like this:

1. Principle 2 ("Know what you're trying to do") and Principle 7 ("Look at things from others' points of view") enable us to understand precisely the (mutual) problem that we're trying to solve. We might not particularly like the person with whom we are negotiating, but we can see his or her viewpoint. We can see that to get a wise agreement, that viewpoint has to be taken into account. Principle 7 gives us the capability to gather all of the relevant data about the issue being negotiated. We don't just get to understand people's bargaining positions. Instead, we see the much wider picture of their interests—the things that are important to them and must form part of the final agreement. Having discovered and gathered together all of this information, we are now in a position to understand completely the issue we are trying to address (Principle 2).

2. When we looked at Principle 3 ("There is always a sequence of events"), we talked about how there always has to be another way. Rather than coming up with just one solution and arguing about that, identify a range of possible solutions to the problem. Make it an exercise in creativity rather than a match full of negativity. Keep asking if there are other ways to solve the problem.

3. Either the chosen solution is fair or it isn't (Principle 6, "Things either are or they aren't"). Either it satisfies the interests of all the negotiating parties or it doesn't. By using some objective measure (e.g., equal treatment, equal pain, expert opinion, market value, precedent), we have a way of deciding whether things are or aren't acceptable to all parties.

Example 41: Presentations

You know how busy you are. Everyone else is that busy, too, with never enough time and so many things to be done. Now, if people are going to give up some of their incredibly scarce time to come and listen to something you have to say, then you better make sure it's worth listening to.

In my experience, good presentations are something of a rarity. Instead I've seen plenty of presenters and presentations that were smug, patronizing, overaggressive, incomprehensible, unconvincing, rambling, scared, verbose, too longwinded, boring, too casual, dishonest, or unsure. The presenter who is authoritative, interesting, relaxed, maybe humorous or dramatic, who believes in what he says, and who communicates that belief, is still something of an oasis in the desert.

Although you'll always learn something useful at them, you don't have to have attended umpteen presentation skills courses to be a good presenter. Common sense shows you what you have to do to make a good presentation.

1. Principle 7 ("Look at things from others' points of view") starts us in the right place. People are going to give up their time to come to this presentation. Why is that going to be a useful thing for them to do? Presumably they're going to learn something that is to their advantage. But, you might say, "I'm making a sales presentation, I'm trying to sell them something, not educate them." I don't think so. I make sales presentations all the time, and the best ones are those where I, first of all, set out to teach my audience something, and then somewhere in the midst of it all, I put in the sales messages. How many pure sales presentations have you been to that you remember? You must tell them something that is to their advantage, or they won't remember your presentation either. If at all possible, ask members of the audience some time in advance of the presentation what they are hoping to get from it. This obviously maximizes the chances that you will actually give

them that. You can do this right up to the moment you're about to begin; however, the earlier you do it, the more time you have to prepare.

2. Principle 2 ("Know what you're trying to do") has helped you decided you're going to tell your audience something to their advantage. Now you need to decide precisely what your main messages are. Because it is a well-known fact that people can't remember too many things, you'd better make sure that you only have a handful of main messages.

3. Principle 3 ("There is always a sequence of events") helps you now decide the sequence in which you are going to tell your audience the messages. Research has shown that the human brain primarily remembers the following:

- Items from the beginning of the learning period (the primacy effect)

- Items from the end of the learning period (the recency effect)

- Items that are emphasized as being in some way outstanding or unique

Of course, you didn't need research to tell you this. It's known through the great adage for all presenters:

- Tell them what you're going to tell them.

- Tell them.

- Tell them what you told them.

Again, research has shown that people remember those items of particular interest to them; hence the value of understanding in advance what it is they want to know. This also tells us that we should try to present each of our points from a point of view that our listeners can relate to (Principle 7, "Look at things from others' points of view").

4. Principle 5 ("Things rarely turn out as expected") will help you anticipate the questions that might get asked. If you can't, have a dry run—this will bring them up anyway. Questions can often take you down paths you hadn't intended to go and deliver messages you didn't intend to deliver. A dry run will help you spot these trap doors and close them. Questions also highlight points where your presentation is weak or prone to misunderstanding, so they are invaluable in terms of improving the presentation next time you give it. Of course, that is if you view questions in this way—as a learning opportunity. Not everyone does!

5. Now go do it. Use the adage of first things first to deliver your key messages at the beginning. Work your way through the rest of it. Then remind the audience of the key messages at the end.

Example 42: Common-Sense Selling

Before I had to do it myself, I was terrified of selling. The notion that I would be put in a situation where I would have to sweet-talk somebody into parting with money filled me with dread. These days I regard it as no big deal. In fact, I quite enjoy the sense of achievement that comes with having done it well—on the rare occasions when I do!

The key to selling is that people must want to buy. The key to this is that they must have a problem that can be solved by what you are selling. How then do you go about selling something to somebody? (Notice, too, that in what follows our analysis unfolds as a sequence of events; i.e., we are using Principle 3.)

1. Principle 2 ("Know what you're trying to do") gets us started. What are we trying to sell? In the jargon, we must have product knowledge. We must know all about what our thing does (its features), how it works, and why what it does is of value to people (its benefits). The benefits are the most important. Why would

anybody in his or her right mind want to buy it? What will it do for them? How will it improve their lives? Too often, people sell features and not benefits. We must know how our thing fits with related things, either sold by us or sold by our competitors. We must know all about how it is delivered. We must know its pricing. If we ask ourselves (Principle 1, "Many things are simple") a few simple questions (What? Where? When? Why? How?), it will generally enable us to winkle out all we need to know by way of product knowledge.

2. Knowing what we're trying to sell, we must now find some people to sell it to. The people who will buy this particular thing you are selling are the people who (a) have the problem you have identified, and (b) have the money to spend on your solution. There will be certain types of people more likely to buy than others. Indeed there will be an ideal customer—a customer who has exactly the problems you are trying to solve and the money to pay for your solution. Once you have identified these customer characteristics, you can start looking among the general population for these people. Advertising, direct mail, cold calling, referrals, and your own contacts will enable you to find these people. The customer characteristics will enable you to gauge how likely or not a person is to buy (i.e., how hot the lead is). A potential customer who has almost all of the characteristics is obviously more likely to buy than one who only has one or two.

3. Now that you've identified a likely target, you need to go sell to them. One way or another you need to get in front of them. In some cases—say, if you open a shop—they will come to you (at least you hope they will). Otherwise, you will have to find a way of going to them. You might have advertised, direct mailed, followed up direct mail with a phone call, had a referral, or made a cold call, but in all cases, the net result of what you have done needs to be that you have arranged some form of meeting. At the

meeting, your aim is to establish that the customer does indeed have the problem that you can solve. Sometimes they will tell you; sometimes you will have to dig it out of them. The important thing here is not to jump in with your solution too soon [11]. Otherwise, you might end up solving the wrong problem or not solving the problem at all. Use Principle 7 ("Look at things from others' points of view"). Pretend you are in their job, their situation; see the things they are describing; try to understand why the things they are describing are such a problem; and try to make connections (Principle 3, "There is always a sequence of events") between the various aspects of the problem they describe. Play things back to them (e.g., "So this means that when this happens, you have this problem, but that must mean that sometimes this must occur") to show that you understand their problem. Try to get a sense of what this problem is costing them in financial terms. This will also often have the effect of clarifying the problem for the customer. Try to think of yourself less as a salesman during this part than as a consultant. If you can teach them something and give away some free hints and tips (without giving away the shop, obviously), so much the better.

4. Now tell your story. Either your solution solves the problem or it doesn't (Principle 6, "Things either are or they aren't"). If it doesn't, walk away. Attempting to bluff, you'll be found out sooner or later. If it does—and if you've done Steps 1 through 3 properly, this should be the case—present your solution. Show how the various aspects of your solution attack and solve the various elements of the customer's problem. Show how your solution has solved similar problems for similar customers. Encourage questions, just in case there are other parts of the problem that you failed to unearth. Encourage objections. These show you where you have missed parts of the problem analysis. Not only are they important for that particular sale, but they enable you to improve your problem analysis and presentation in the future, so that you don't

encounter these particular objections again. Used in this way, objections become a vital part of improving your sales technique and results. Finally, if it's feasible, demonstrate your solution in action.

5. There have been studies done that indicate that the single biggest reason that people fail to sell something is that they fail to ask for the order! However distasteful you might find this, you must do it. If you've successfully unearthed the customer's needs and problems and shown that what you have will satisfy those needs and solve those problems, then it only remains for you to ask if you now have a deal. At this stage you might end up doing another lap around some more objections, which could include objections to the price. That is why it's useful to understand the cost of the problem in the first place. If you fail to get a deal on price, there are two possibilities: Either you are too expensive or you were never going to get the deal in the first place and the price is just being used as an excuse. Because pricing is something of an art, this is always a somewhat tricky question. Losing some deals on price is not a bad thing, because it means you are not pricing too cheaply. On the other hand, you don't want to lose too many. I've seen a figure of 10 percent of deals lost because of price proposed and that seems reasonable enough to me.

6. Principle 3 ("There is always a sequence of events") gets us through the final steps of the sale. What has to happen now? Who will do what to ensure that the necessary paperwork goes back and forth, the required arrangements are made, and the product or service is delivered?

So What Should You Do?

1. When you are undertaking anything, remember that in almost all cases, other people will be affected by what you do. See if you can ensure that you identify who those people are, what their views and needs are, and how much you can take these into account.

2. The first point isn't just something you do at the beginning of the undertaking and then ignore after that. You must remain conscious of and sensitive to it over the life of the venture.

3. If at all possible, when planning something, try to involve the people who will do the work.

PRINCIPLE 1: MANY THINGS ARE SIMPLE

PRINCIPLE 2: KNOW WHAT YOU'RE TRYING TO DO

PRINCIPLE 3: THERE IS ALWAYS A SEQUENCE OF EVENTS

PRINCIPLE 4: THINGS DON'T GET DONE IF PEOPLE DON'T DO THEM

PRINCIPLE 5: THINGS RARELY TURN OUT AS EXPECTED

PRINCIPLE 6: THINGS EITHER ARE OR THEY AREN'T

PRINCIPLE 7: LOOK AT THINGS FROM OTHERS' POINTS OF VIEW

References

1. Wouk, Herman, *This Is My God*, Boston: Little, Brown & Co., 1988, p. 38.

2.–3. His Holiness The Dalai Lama and Cutler, Howard C., *The Art of Happiness*, New York: Riverhead Books, 1998, p. 89.

4. Covey, Stephen R., *The 7 Habits of Highly Effective People*, New York: Simon & Schuster, 1990.

5. Milne, A. A., *The House at Pooh Corner*, London: Egmont Books, 1974, p. 9.

6.–7. Buzan, Tony with Buzan, Barry, *The Mind Map Book*, New York: Plume/Penguin, 1993.

8.–9. Schwartz, Nelson D., "Secrets of Fortune's Fastest-Growing Companies," *Fortune*, September 6, 1999, p. 72.

10. Fisher, Roger and Ury, William, *Getting to Yes*, London: Random House, 1999, p. 4.

11. Winkler, John, *Winning Sales and Marketing Tactics*, Oxford, England: Butterworth Heinemann, 1989.

AFTERWORD

Remembering Common Sense (Part 1)

I've tried, in the course of the book, to keep reminding you of the seven principles of common sense. Here is another way to think about them:

- Principles 1 and 7 can be thought of as overarching principles. Keep things simple and see them from other viewpoints.

- Principle 2 is about knowing what you're trying to achieve.

- Principles 3 through 6 are built around the sequence of events, which is how we accomplish what it is we're trying to achieve.

Remembering Common Sense (Part 2)

1. In general, rather than looking for complicated ways to do things, we're going to do the opposite. (Principle 1, "Many things are simple.")

2. In considering any venture, undertaking, or project, we need to understand what it is we're trying to do. (Principle 2, "Know what you're trying to do.")

3. Once we know what we're trying to do, Principle 3 ("There is always a sequence of events") guides us through doing it.

4. The sequence of events happens only if people do the jobs in the sequence. (Principle 4, "Things don't get done if people don't do them.")

5. No matter how well thought out the sequence of events is, there are always surprises. (Principle 5, "Things rarely turn out as expected.")

6. As our sequence of events unfolds, jobs in the sequence are either complete or they are not. (Principle 6, "Things either are or they aren't.")

7. As well as keeping things simple, we should always consider various viewpoints. (Principle 7, "Look at things from others' points of view.")

Practicing Common Sense (Part 1)

It's all been a bit pointless—me writing this book and you reading it, I mean—if you don't do something as a result. Conveniently, because it wasn't deliberate on my part, we have ended up with seven principles of common sense. Thus, one way you could begin to remember them and, more important, to apply them, would be to concentrate on a different one each day of the week.

- Mondays, focus on Principle 1, "Many things are simple." You could focus on trying to keep things simple. Try to plan for an uncomplicated day with less rushing around than normal. At meetings, if things look like they're getting too complicated, drag the participants back to a simpler view of things. Ask yourself constantly if things are as simple as they could be. Perhaps extend the simplicity to other areas of your life—what you wear, what you eat, how you get to work, how much garbage you generate, or how much of the world's resources you use. Find a simple pleasure that you enjoy and make space for it in the day. Take something that you normally do that day and try to find a simpler way of doing it. Try something off the "So What Should You Do?" list at the end of Chapter 1.

- Tuesdays, focus on Principle 2, "Know what you're trying to do." Have an objective that you're trying to achieve today and achieve it no matter what. For any meetings you go to, calls you make, or presentations you give, understand in advance what you're hoping to get from them. Review at the end of the day how you did. Try something off the "So What Should You Do?" list at the end of Chapter 2.

- Wednesdays, focus on Principle 3, "There is always a sequence of events." Think in terms of sequences of events. Do the things you intend to do today align with the bigger goals you have identified for yourself? Are the jobs you intend to do today taken from the stacks of your various undertakings? After meetings, calls, or conversations, ensure that things aren't left hanging, but that everybody is clear about what is going to happen next. Try something off the "So What Should You Do?" list at the end of Chapter 3.

- Thursdays, focus on Principle 4, "Things don't get done if people don't do them." From a personal point of view, focus on finishing the things you intended to get done. Review how you fared at the end of the day. How did things actually pan out? Did you achieve what you set out to achieve, or did other things intervene? If the latter, what can you learn from today and what can you do to ensure that this doesn't happen to you again? If you have people doing things for you, are they clear on what needs to be done? Are you happy that they've thought through their sequences of events and have ample time to do what they've promised? Use dance cards with them if they're having problems, because their problems will eventually become your problems. Try something off the "So What Should You Do?" list at the end of Chapter 4.

- Fridays, focus on Principle 5, "Things rarely turn out as expected." Ask yourself if there are contingencies in place on all of your key projects. Have you done a risk analysis on them? If not, do one. If you have, review your Top 10 Risks lists and see if you're doing all you can to mitigate them. Try something off the "So What Should You Do?" list at the end of Chapter 5.

- Saturdays, focus on Principle 6, "Things either are or they aren't." If you're at home, then this will probably raise questions about the status of that do-it-yourself job that's been outstanding for a long time, or something in the garden, or the washing or the cooking for next week, or the homework assignment for the course you're taking, or things to do with the children. If you've chosen the five-day common-sense week, then keep the focus on whether things are really done; and if people are claiming they are done, how can they prove it. Try something off the "So What Should You Do?" list at the end of Chapter 6.

- Sundays, focus on Principle 7, "Look at things from others' points of view." This is not a bad thing to do any day of the week. Spend a little time seeing the world as somebody else sees it—your partner, child, parent, employer, boss, subordinate, team member, peer, work colleague, family member, or friend. You might be surprised by what you'll learn. Try something off the "So What Should You Do?" list at the end of Chapter 7.

Finally, good luck!

Practicing Common Sense (Part 2)

Principles 1 ("Know what you're trying to do) and 2 ("There is always a sequence of events") provide a *very* powerful way of tackling any problem. We saw this at work in Chapter 7, Example 42. Establish what it is you're trying to do using Principle 1. Now ask yourself— using Principle 2—what the starting point is. What is the first job in the sequence of events? In Example 42, we established that it was to fig-ure out what it was we were trying to sell. Again using Principle 2, ask yourself what happens next. What's the next job in the sequence of events, the next link in the chain? As you identify each job, some of our principles might offer further insights.

Carry on like this until you have established an unbroken sequence of jobs from where you are now to where you want to be.

BIBLIOGRAPHY

Apart from the references at the end of individual chapters, the following books were also consulted during the writing of this book.

1. Chopra, Deepak, *The Seven Spiritual Laws of Success*, San Francisco: Amber-Allen, 1995.

2. Gladwell, Malcolm, *The Tipping Point—How Little Things Can Make A Big Difference*, Boston: Back Bay Books, 2002.

3. His Holiness The Dalai Lama, *Ancient Wisdom, Modern World*, London: Little Brown, 1999.

4. Hoff, Benjamin, *The Tao of Pooh & The Te of Piglet*, New York: Penguin USA, 1993.

5. Kellaway, Lucy, *Sense and Nonesense in the Office*, London: Financial Times Prentice Hall, 2000.

6. Lovell, Jim and Kluger, Jeffrey, *Apollo 13*, New York: Pocket Books, 1994.

7. O'Connell, Fergus, *How to Run Successful Projects II—The Silver Bullet,* Hemel Hempstead, England: Prentice Hall, 1996.

8. Schumacher, E. F., *Small Is Beautiful: Economics As If People Mattered*, London: HarperCollins, 1989.

INDEX

ABOUT THE AUTHOR

The Sunday Business Post has described **Fergus O'Connell** as having "more strings to his bow than a Stradivarius." He has a First in Mathematical Physics and has worked in information technology, software development, and general management with companies such as CPT, ICL, and Retix. In 1992, he founded ETP (*www.etpint.com*), which is now one of the world's leading program and project management companies. His experience covers projects around the world; he has taught project management in Europe, North America, South America, and the Far East.

O'Connell is the author of five books:

- *How to Run Successful Projects—The Silver Bullet* [Third edition, Addison-Wesley, 2001]

- *How to Run Successful High-Tech Project-Based Organizations* [Artech House, 1999]

- *How to Run Successful Projects in Web-Time* [Artech House, 2000]

- *Simply Brilliant—The Competitive Advantage of Common Sense* [Financial Times Prentice Hall, 2001]

- *Call the Swallow* [The Collins Press, March 2002]

The first of these, sometimes simply known as *The Silver Bullet*, has become both a bestseller and a classic. *Simply Brilliant*—also a bestseller—was runner-up in the WH Smith Book Awards in 2002. *Call the Swallow* was short-listed for the 2002 Kerry Ingredients Irish Fiction Prize. His books have been translated into seven languages.

O'Connell has written on project management for *The Sunday Business Post*, *Computer Weekly*, and *The Wall Street Journal*. He has lectured on project management at University College Cork, Bentley College, Boston University, the Michael Smurfit Graduate School of Business, and on television for the National Technological University.

He has two children and lives in Ireland.

Notes

Notes

Notes

Notes

Notes

Notes

Notes

Notes

Notes

Notes

Notes

Notes

8 reasons why you should read the Financial Times for 4 weeks RISK-FREE!

To help you stay current with significant
developments in the world economy ...
and to assist you to make informed business
decisions — the Financial Times brings you:

❶ Fast, meaningful overviews of international affairs ... plus daily briefings on major world news.

❷ Perceptive coverage of economic, business, financial and political developments with special focus on emerging markets.

❸ More international business news than any other publication.

❹ Sophisticated financial analysis and commentary on world market activity plus stock quotes from over 30 countries.

❺ Reports on international companies and a section on global investing.

❻ Specialized pages on management, marketing, advertising and technological innovations from all parts of the world.

❼ Highly valued single-topic special reports (over 200 annually) on countries, industries, investment opportunities, technology and more.

❽ The Saturday Weekend FT section — a globetrotter's guide to leisure-time activities around the world: the arts, fine dining, travel, sports and more.

FT FINANCIAL TIMES
World business newspaper